Making Mentoring Happen

**A simple and effective guide
to implementing
a successful mentoring program**

Business &
Professional
Publishing
Pty Limited

Business & Professional Publishing Pty Limited
Unit 7/5 Vuko Place
Warriewood NSW 2102

Email: info@woodslane.com.au

First published 1999
Reprinted 2000, 2001 (three times), 2004

National Library of Australia
Cataloguing-in-Publication Data

Lacey, Kathy,
    Making mentoring happen: a simple and effective guide to implementing a successful mentoring program.

    ISBN 1 875680 68 3.
    1. Mentoring in the professions. 2. Mentoring in business.
    I. Title.

371.102

Publisher: Tim Edwards
Distributed in Australia and New Zealand by Woodslane Pty Limited
Printed in Australia by McPherson's Printing Group

Business & Professional Publishing publications are available through booksellers and other resellers. For further information contact Woodslane Australia on +61 2 9970 5111 or email info@woodslane.com.au

Making It Happen

Are you committed to changing things for the better? Are you searching for ways to make your organisation more effective? Are you trying to help your people and organisation to improve, but are seriously strapped for time and money? If you are, then this Making It Happen book is written specifically for you.

Every book in the series is designed to assist change agents to get things done ... to make new programs really happen ... without costing the organisation an arm and a leg and without taking up all of your valuable time.

Every book is written by a top consultant in the field who does not simply theorize about their subject of expertise but who explains specifically how to implement a program that will really work for your work unit or organisation. Vital advice on what works and what doesn't work, what tricks to implement and traps to avoid, plus suggested programs and strategies for implementation, templates and material to photocopy—each book in the series is filled with useful information such as this, all written in clear, practical language that enables you to make things happen, fast.

Help your people and work unit to increase their performance and love their work through implementing a program from the Making It Happen series and reap the rewards that successful change agents deserve.

ABOUT THE BOOK

The mentoring process involves at least two people: a mentor and a protégé (or mentee). The mentor uses their greater knowledge, expertise and experience to help the protégé develop their own skills. While the protégé receives obvious benefits from the relationship, the mentor too is rewarded, both personally and professionally. Organisations also benefit from the increased efficiency of their staff.

So, although mentoring may occur spontaneously with excellent results, it makes sense for progressive organisations to actively promote the mentoring process. Making Mentoring Happen does just what it says; first by explaining the concept of mentoring and outlining the benefits for all those involved; then by showing the details of how a program can be implemented; finally by providing the training activities and sample documents that make the program run smoothly.

Whether a business wants to reduce staff turnover, induct new employees more successfully, fast-track their best employees, increase the skills of particular groups of employees, make best use of their senior staff and keep them motivated, or improve company performance and morale, a mentoring program will help. Making Mentoring Happen shows how easy it is to set up a mentoring program that really works to everyone's benefit.

Kathy Lacey MEd, Grad Dip TESOL, Dip of Primary Teaching is a practising consultant who specialises in mentoring programs and has successfully developed mentoring programs for clients such as the Victorian Department of Education. Kathy is the owner of the Melbourne company, Right Angles Consulting Pty Limited and has successfully published on Performance Appraisal and Educational Theory.

CONTENTS

ABOUT THE SERIES   iii

ABOUT THE BOOK   v

ABOUT THE AUTHOR   v

CHAPTER ONE   **Developments in Mentoring**   **1**

Formal Mentoring Programs   3

Organisational Needs   4

Employee Needs   6

Some Useful Definitions   6

Professional Supporters   8

Role of the Mentor   12

Role of the Mentee   13

Benefits of Mentoring Programs   13

CHAPTER TWO   **How Mentoring Works**   **17**

Types of Mentoring   17

Mentoring Functions   18

Program Characteristics   21

A Formal Mentoring Program in a Nutshell   21

Potential Pitfalls   32

CHAPTER THREE   **Mentoring in the Workplace**   **35**

Perceptions of Learners   *35*
Developing Strong Mentor Relationships   *38*
Role of the Facilitator in the Relationship   *43*
Factors that Influence the Decline of the Relationship   *45*
Behaviours that Help the Relationship to Mature   *45*

CHAPTER FOUR   **Program Design**   **48**

Training Support   *49*
Orientation   *49*
Mid-Cycle   *55*
Relationship Closure   *55*
Final Recommendations   *56*

CHAPTER FIVE   **Activities**   **58**

Orientation   *58*
Mid-Cycle   *88*
Relationship Closure   *99*

CHAPTER SIX   **Additional Program Material**   **102**

Checklists   *102*
Sample Documents   *108*
Proformas   *115*
Other Tools   *122*

Developments in Mentoring

Formal Mentoring Programs ● **Organisational Needs** ●
Employee Needs ● **Some Useful Definitions** ● **Professional**
Supporters ● **Role of the Mentor** ● **Role of the Mentee** ●
Benefits of Mentoring Programs

'What lies behind us and what lies before us are tiny matters compared to what lies within us.' Oliver Wendell Holmes

Mentoring is like constructing footbridges. The mentor is the engineer, designing and constructing different bridges as people and conditions change. Sometimes mentors will need to construct wide, solid bridges with handrails and very limited risk to help mentees move towards new experiences. At other times their partners will be ready and only need a little encouragement to use a narrow suspension bridge swaying in gale-force winds—with planks missing and little or no handrails.

A wise mentor will spend time getting to know their partner and the path that they want to follow. The mentor acts as a guide and support along that journey, sometimes building bridges, sometimes encouraging the mentee to use less secure bridges, cross unknown territory and eventually to forge out on their own.

A few years ago I came across the following tale. It reminds me very much of the mentoring experience and illustrates a number of lessons.

The Bridge

A blind man lived in a small town deep in the mountains. He was not afraid of the mountain paths, which he had known since childhood. He regularly visited his brother who lived in another small town not far away but separated by a deep gorge. When spring came and the snows melted he used to pride himself on being the first to go across the gorge. There was a small footbridge across it, consisting of three wide planks driven into the earth on either side, with a small wooden handrail.

One autumn, when the blind man made his last trip before winter, he noticed that the planks were becoming shaky, because the earth was crumbling away. He mentioned this to the mayor, who saw the government inspectors on their next round. The latter promised that the bridge would be repaired for the next spring.

When spring came, the blind man had a mild illness which kept him in bed for a week. The post office sent a telegram to the brother so that he would not worry. When the blind man was well again they sent another, saying that he would definitely pay a visit the next day.

He set out feeling the warmth of the spring sun; walking confidently until he came to the bridge. He moved down the little steps cut into the earth, and felt for the bridge with his foot. To his horror he found that there was now only one shaky plank, and no handrail at all. He realised that the old bridge had not been repaired and, even worse, a winter storm must have carried most of it away. However, he had sent his telegram and he was too proud to turn back. He got down on all fours and crawled across, sweating as he heard the cataract below.

When he got to the other side and arrived at his brother's home he told his story.

'But the bridge has been repaired,' said his brother, and they went back together. His brother told him, 'The new bridge is a splendid one, driven into the solid rock just below the old bridge. It's been newly painted. There is a sign up on the bank saying "Till the paint is dry, please use the plank which has been left for you." Of course the engineers knew that anyone could easily walk across the plank.'

'Yes,' groaned the blind man. 'Easy if you know that there's a wide bridge just below. But if you don't, it's all you can do to wriggle across, clinging tightly to the plank, and pouring sweat with each movement.'

When we start working for a different company, or take on new responsibilities, how often do we feel blind or as if we are operating in the dark? We fear the unknown, often assuming the worst, and lose confidence. It's easy if we know there is guidance at hand. Just knowing it's there provides the boost to our confidence that means we probably won't need to call on it.

A possible moral for this story—'Don't make assumptions'—provides the following important messages for mentors and their partners.

- Don't assume that there is no guidance or help.
- Don't assume that people know there is help available.
- Don't assume that everyone sees things as you do. What's easy for some will be hard for others.

Formal Mentoring Programs

This book is about structured mentoring programs. Over the past five years I have been heavily involved in the development, facilitation and evaluation of mentoring programs. In 1996 I completed my Master of Education at the University of Melbourne. Mentoring programs were the focus of my research. In particular, I tracked the participants in one of my mentoring programs from their initial expressions of interest to twelve months after the formal conclusion of the program. Since then I have developed other mentoring programs and conducted the training for a range of other mentoring-type programs. This book is the culmination of that work. Chapters One, Two and Three explore the issues to do with mentoring programs such as definitions, program designs, selecting, matching and training participants, supporting relationships and finally concluding the formal relationship. Chapters Four, Five and Six are written for people wishing to develop their own local mentoring program. They provide a wealth of practical ideas to enable any manager to establish, maintain and evaluate an effective program. Sample training activities and proformas are included. These will need minimal adaptation to suit individual cases. Throughout the book I have quoted from interviews and written evaluations of mentors, mentees and managers of various programs in which I have been involved.

There have been both formal and informal mentoring relationships in the past; the concept of mentoring is an ancient one. The story of Mentor comes from Homer's *Odyssey*. When Odysseus, King of Ithaca, went to fight in the Trojan War he entrusted the care of his household to Mentor. Mentor served as a teacher and overseer to Odysseus' son, Telemachus. (We are left to ponder why Penelope, Odysseus' wife, was not considered suitable!) After the war, Odysseus was condemned to wander vainly for ten years in his attempt to return home. Telemachus, now grown, went in search of his father. Telemachus was accompanied on his quest by Athena, goddess of war and patroness of the arts and industry. At this time Athena assumed the form of Mentor. Eventually father and son were reunited. In time, the word mentor came to mean trusted advisor, friend, teacher, wise person.

The relationship between Mentor and Telemachus was a formal one. Odysseus requested Mentor to take on the role and established the parameters of the relationship. Informal mentoring relationships, on the other hand, begin spontaneously and are not based on stated expectations of each other's role.

Current formal mentoring programs have strong links to Odysseus' model of the mentor being like a family friend, providing long-term guidance and counsel. The mentor is a facilitator of learning rather than a teacher of tricks. The program designer and facilitator is like Odysseus—selecting appropriate pairs, briefing them on the expectations of the relationship and ensuring that the mentor has the appropriate interpersonal skills.

In the past some organisations have been reluctant to formalise mentoring relationships, believing that 'true' mentoring only occurred spontaneously. There was a belief that informal mentoring relies on personal choice of partner, personality congruence and luck. Others believed that targeted, structured programs with custom-designed goals and activities have the advantage of identifying all participants who can benefit from mentoring, rather than relying on like people finding one another. It is not an either/or debate. Informal mentoring will continue. Organisations are advised to develop cultures where spontaneous mentor relationships develop and are supported. Formal mentor relationships based on some choice of partner will broaden the number of employees who can access these programs and realise their benefits.

Recently, there has been increased interest in mentoring as a management development strategy in both education and industry. Both sectors have recognised the importance of life-long learning and the development of the attitude of establishing the workplace as a learning organisation. The Report of the Industry Task Force on Leadership and Management Skills in 1995 (often referred to as the Karpin Report) states that as the business environment changes, so do the skills and characteristics required of managers. The typical manager will need to become the leader/enabler within a learning organisation. Training program designers have recognised that people learn best when they learn from each other in workplace settings rather than through structured courses at specialised training facilities.

Organisational needs

Organisations are constantly looking for solutions to a number of human resource concerns and professional development needs. Mentoring processes will meet many human resource needs, but beware of asking too much of any one program. Design programs to meet one specific need. In some cases your program will meet some of your other needs simultaneously, but don't count on it. If you try to design a program that meets multiple needs you can be pretty well guaranteed that it will meet none of them.

Mentoring programs can be used for the following purposes.

Induction of new staff

Identifying appropriate new staff is a costly exercise. Organisations wish to reduce this cost as far as possible by ensuring that new employees are supported and inducted quickly into 'our way of doing things'. Mentors provide excellent role models and coaches for new employees. In one company, staff retention rates improved quite dramatically after a mentoring program for new employees was introduced.

Succession planning

Hiring new staff at any level is a costly exercise that can also be a gamble. Many organisations prefer a policy of promoting from within wherever possible. Human resource personnel need to provide internal programs that identify and provide skills training for potential leaders. One company now has a policy of promoting from within wherever possible. Mentors and managers are expected to identify suitable candidates for fast tracking.

Support for potential leaders from minority or under-represented groups

There are groups that are under-represented in leadership positions in most workplaces. In some cases organisations have a legislative responsibility to improve this situation. Many organisations also realise the benefits of diversity at all levels in the workplace. Mentoring has been used to support aspirant women leaders, managers and directors, particularly through shadowing programs.

Support for isolated employees

These days employees can be required to work alone or unsupported for reasons beyond geographic isolation. The increased use of technology has meant that it is not unusual to find employees working from home-based offices, communicating with the 'office' electronically. They may never, or only infrequently, meet with colleagues or managers face to face. In the down-sized (now often referred to as right-sized) organisation, employees have fewer colleagues to call on for advice and support.

Provide incentive for high fliers

Having carefully selected their new employee, organisations want to maintain the motivation of the high-fliers to stay within their organisation. Ambitious good performers might be capable of accelerating by leaps and bounds up the promotion ladder. If there is no possibility of this occurring within their organisation they will look to move from one company or business to another to achieve their goals. One small publishing house recognised this problem after a succession of bright young staff members resigned to take promotions elsewhere. Early counselling through a mentoring program turned this around.

Reduce burnout

Managers and leaders who have been with one organisation for some time are often looking for a career challenge. They may not be looking for promotion but a new direction or renewed motivation. They are valuable employees with a wealth of intellectual property and experiences that could usefully be passed on to the current generation of new leaders.

Supporting an organisational learning philosophy

Increasingly, leaders within organisations are seeing the benefits of the continuous learning cycle. Businesses that are thriving in a constantly changing environment have a culture that encourages learning at all levels in the organisation. Employees are encouraged to develop the ability to control and reflect on their learning and thinking processes. Everyone in the organisation is expected to use a range of thinking skills from low level (recall) to high level (analysis, synthesis, evaluation). Employees are prepared to take risks, are confident and knowledgeable about their abilities, and are intrinsically motivated to improve their own performance. They have the persistence and self-discipline required to concentrate on initiating and working through their own learning plan.

Employee needs

The following groups of employees will gain from mentoring programs.

Induction

Staff new to the organisation or new to a particular position within the organisation. A mentee new to a senior management role commented to me that prior to the mentor program they often felt overwhelmed, and just hoped that many decisions they made were the right ones. Now if they are unsure they have a trusted friend in their mentor that they run the decision by. In most cases they haven't changed how they handle the situation, they just feel more confident about their decisions.

Aspirant

Employees who aspire to leadership positions within the organisation and demonstrate the potential to develop the skills to enable them to perform leadership roles.

Fast tracking

Employees who demonstrate potential to perform several levels above their current level and have the ability to develop the necessary skills very rapidly. These employees also need a fast track method of gaining a broad base of work experiences.

Experienced leaders

Current managers and leaders within the organisation who might have been in these positions for some time. They are excellent corporate models, with a wealth of experience but are looking for a new challenge. If their organisation does not provide the challenge they may well look elsewhere for it.

Some useful definitions

What exactly is a mentor or a mentee? What are their roles? How is a mentor different to a coach? How many mentors can I have? Are there any other roles that professional supporters play? Do I need all of these people? We need to answer these and other questions relating to defining who and what we are talking about before we go much further.

A mentor is a trusted and significant leader who works with a partner (a mentee) to help them learn things more quickly or earlier, or to learn things they otherwise might not have learnt. The relationship is long term and based, from the very beginning, on free choice to continue the relationship.

Formal mentoring programs provide a structure to support the deliberate pairing of the more skilled and experienced person with the less skilled and experienced person. The mentor is seen as having a breadth and depth of experience that the mentee could not have had at this stage of their career. The purpose of the relationship is to develop the mentee's unique skills and abilities, not to make a clone of the mentor.

Mentoring can include providing emotional and psychological support; direct assistance with professional development; and role modelling. Mentors will find that they will start off providing one or two components of support, usually beginning with role modelling. By the conclusion of the formal program most mentors will have provided each component at various stages of the relationship.

Mentors in programs specifically established to support staff members new to an organisation, or those new to leadership positions, are frequently asked to provide **emotional and psychological support**. The new employee, and particularly the new leader, will go through periods of uncertainty and lack confidence. A staff member new to a position, regardless of the level, is unlikely to share their feelings of uncertainty with their peers, manager or team members. The mentor may be the only professional person with whom they can share these feelings, admit that they haven't got a clue what to do or simply that the going is tough. The mentor plays a key role in supporting the mentee by listening to their concerns and providing encouragement. One of the most powerful things that a mentor can do for a mentee is to believe in them and encourage them.

Mentoring programs specifically designed to support aspiring leaders require the mentor to provide direct assistance with **professional development** planning. The mentor will often work with the mentee to identify their professional strengths and weaknesses. There are a lot of tools available to help the pair to appraise the mentee's current level of performance. Some of these tools have been described in Chapters Four, Five and Six. The mentor can assist the mentee to develop an action plan to build on the strengths and address the weaknesses. There are real benefits in having a mentor assist in the development of this plan. Plans developed by the mentee alone usually lack direction, are often superficial and not related to a rigorous performance appraisal. The mentor helps to provide the motivation to develop the plan, helps to focus the plan and provides critical feedback that will ensure that the plan is rigorous and relates to the mentee's skills and needs. Another benefit of involving the mentor in the development and implementation of a plan for career enhancement is that the mentee then has access to the mentor's professional network. The mentor can introduce the mentee to people with specific skills to act as coaches, and provide opportunities for the mentee to take on tasks and projects that will extend their expertise, with the help of a strong support structure to ensure that the project will not fail. The mentor also acts as a sponsor, promoting the mentee's skills in important forums.

Mentees at all levels will benefit from observing a skilled manager in operation. The mentor provides a role model of the skills, knowledge and attitudes valued by the organisation. Such observation also provides a unique opportunity to then discuss aspects such as how the mentor gained these skills, the gap between the mentor's skills and the mentee's and how the mentee might develop their skills.

Structured mentoring programs can be based on just the professional growth of the mentee or the personal and professional growth of the mentee. Successful mentoring relationships from programs that emphasise just the professional aspects of the mentee's growth and development often end up also providing personal support and counselling.

Definitions of mentors agree that the mentor acts as a professional guide because of their greater experience. Mentors may also be able to assist mentees because of their position, status or performance.

Professional supporters

When most of us reflect on our career development we discover that many people have played different roles in our personal and professional development. It is hard to actually categorise some of these roles. Most of us can identify role models and coaches, and we are familiar with the term mentor even if we have not been fortunate enough to have worked with a mentor. In my own past I have worked with people that I would now describe as informal mentors or sponsors. They provided emotional and psychological support, direct assistance with my career and professional development and role modelling. They also protected, promoted and sponsored me. Because there was no formal structure to the relationship, they were not formal mentors. There were no agreed stated goals of helping me to grow and develop specific competencies, even though this was the outcome of each relationship. It is also doubtful if any of the people involved would have defined themselves as mentors but that is certainly the role that they played.

Activities of Professional Supporters

Supporter	Significant peer	Role model	Coach	Sponsor	Mentor
informal unconscious	informal conscious	informal unconscious	formal conscious	informal unconscious	formal conscious
motivate support	motivate support teach	motivate teach	motivate support teach counsel	motivate support teach counsel promote protect	motivate support teach counsel promote protect

For most of us the other roles outlined below have also been significant, even if we did not realise the significance at the time. The preceding table outlines for each type of supporter the level of formality in the relationship, if the activities are being performed consciously or unconsciously, and the activities being performed by the various professional supporters.

Supporter

A supporter plays an informal role. A supporter is often a colleague and can be working at a similar or more senior level. The key role of the supporter is one of motivation; you might have many different supporters at any one time, providing emotional and psychological support, often unconsciously. The supporter is not consciously motivating you, but that is the effect of their positive feedback and encouragement. A supporter might offer assistance on a day when you are overloaded, offer encouragement or a friendly word when things have gone off the rails a bit, or even cover for you when you're back late from lunch. A supporter is a good team player.

Significant peer

The role of a significant peer is similar to that of a supporter, although peers work at a similar level in the organisation. They work at the same work site or in roles that often require them to work together on projects. They motivate each other and provide psychological and emotional support, on an informal basis, usually subconsciously. You can also have more than one significant peer at any one time. Some of my significant peers found suitable jobs for me to apply for and then encouraged me to apply and supported me through the application process. On other occasions I used these people as a sounding board for ideas or projects that I was working on, or for advice on work-related problems and concerns.

Role model

Your relationship with a role model is an informal one. You can have several role models concurrently. Similarly, someone can unconsciously be a role model for a number of people. Role models provide motivation and teach skills by modelling. They have skills, expertise or hold a position to which we aspire. We have role models at a number of levels. One role model might be a key player in your industry or enterprise, another role model might be a more senior manager or the CEO of your organisation.

Coach

A coach has a formal role, where both parties are aware of each other's role and responsibilities. A coach consciously motivates, models, provides remediation and tutoring in specific skills, offers guidance in the customs of the organisation and can become a confidante. One person might act as a coach to a number of people simultaneously. After making a significant career change I found myself working for a documentation house. I needed to quickly develop computer, desktop publishing and technical writing skills. Fortunately for me, this organisation had some highly skilled personnel who were excellent coaches. I learnt the specific skills through intensive one-to-one training and was given guidance in the customs of the organisation—the way we really do things, which was different to the way the bosses told me that things were done!

Sponsor

Your relationship with a sponsor is an informal one, where roles and responsibilities are not usually discussed or consciously understood. The sponsor would be aware of the person they are sponsoring and what they are doing; but in many cases they would not describe those activities as sponsoring. A sponsor is aware of the activities they are performing on someone else's behalf but the person being sponsored is not always aware of their sponsor or the level of support they are receiving at the time.

Throughout my career I have had the benefit of a couple of influential sponsors. On one occasion, during a major organisational restructure, my then manager was instrumental in my securing a new position. This came to my attention much later during discussions with the manager of the new position. During senior management discussions at the time of the restructure my then manager apparently convinced the potential manager of my transferable skills for the new position. She had not previously known of my skills and I had not been seen as a potential candidate for the position. I was appointed to the position purely on the recommendation of my manager/sponsor.

A sponsor provides introductions to influential people in and beyond the organisation, makes recommendations for promotion, publicly praises accomplishments and abilities, facilitates entry into meetings and activities not normally available to someone at the mentee's level, or offers guidance in the customs of the organisation. They either hold a position of power within the organisation or are held in high regard in the organisation. Managers and leaders within organisations might sponsor many people simultaneously. A sponsor provides motivation subconsciously in the same way as significant peers and role models. They encourage the mentee and demonstrate a belief in their skills and potential, encouraging them to live up to the mentor's expectations. Sponsors play a significant role in larger organisations where they can be more influential. People working in small organisations need to find sponsors from beyond their workplace. Professional associations, service organisations and clubs can provide these networks to allow sponsoring to occur.

Mentor

A mentor offers emotional and psychological support, direct assistance with career and professional development, and role modelling. A mentor oversees the career development of another person through teaching, counselling, providing support, protecting, promoting or sponsoring.

A mentor is part of a formal, one-to-one relationship. Mentors consciously motivate, support, teach, counsel, promote and protect. They provide assistance with career planning. The nature of the relationship means they will often become a confidante and offer personal advice and support, although this may never be formally discussed as part of the role.

At no stage in my career have I had the good fortune to have a formal mentor working with me. However, I have been lucky enough to have an informal mentor adopt me. This occurred when I took up my first leadership position of any significance. My mentor, Tom, was a manager many rungs higher than me and in a different unit—he was not my direct manager. My new position required that I work as Executive Officer for a Task Force that he chaired. Tom recognised my potential but also saw my shortcomings. He provided direct coaching and teaching of skills in the early days, then left me to 'get on with the job', checking in occasionally to see how things were progressing. By the end of the second year of the project he had encouraged me to take on many challenging responsibilities, provided opportunities for me to publicly display my skills and motivated me to apply for promotions.

At any given time people may have a number of supporters, role models and significant peers. Coaches or sponsors may perform their roles for a number of people at the same time whereas a mentor usually performs the role on a one-to-one basis.

Supporters, significant peers, role models and sponsors have an informal relationship. Roles and expectations are not discussed. Coaches and mentors clearly establish roles and expectations. Significant peers, sponsors, supporters and role models play their roles unconsciously. Coaches and mentors are conscious of the activities that they are performing, although they may not define these roles using such formal terms.

The activities performed by sponsors and mentors are identical. A sponsor becomes a mentor by consciously and formally performing these activities in a one-to-one relationship. Mentors clearly establish role definitions and expectations of each party. Both people involved in a mentoring relationship are aware of the relationship and its responsibilities.

Taking time out to consider examples from our past can help us to recognise when we are performing these roles for others and how we can make a significant difference in other people's career development. More important to us, though, is recognising when others might assist in our career development. We need to be able to access professional supporters at all levels of the hierarchy simultaneously. Supporters at the lower end of the hierarchy provide motivation, personal support and specific training. Coaches, sponsors and mentors can also counsel, promote and protect us. These last two functions are particularly important. The term 'promote' is taken here to mean to exert some influence on behalf of the mentee; to talk about their skills in public forums, provide them with access to meetings or activities not normally available to someone at that level. The most highly competent employees will find that their career potential is greatly dependent on those skills being publicly recognised by others. These days it is not enough to just have the skills needed to perform the job—the external perception of our skills by others has an enormous impact on our career development. Mentors and sponsors will often introduce new employees to corporate structures, expectations and taboos. This information is invaluable to the new employee: it is the type of information that is never written and is often only learnt through making innocent mistakes. In this sense they protect the mentee.

Role of the mentor

The role of the mentor will largely be determined by the purpose of the program, which needs to be clearly articulated by the organisation, prior to the selection process. No one person will be a suitable mentor for all programs.

Mentors might be expected to assist the mentee to identify areas for growth and development, provide specific skill training or coaching in these areas, provide psychological support, counselling and advice and eventually to protect and promote the mentee.

They will often be required to:
- encourage the exploration of ideas;
- encourage risk taking in learning;
- listen when the mentee has a problem;
- provide appropriate and timely advice;
- provide appropriate skills training;
- assist the mentee to identify and solve problems;
- help the mentee to shift their mental context; and
- confront negative intentions or behaviours.

At the beginning of the relationship mentors spend most of their time encouraging the mentee, listening, and helping the mentee to identify and solve their own problems. As the relationship grows and they understand each other's style, the mentor will challenge the mentee's perceptions and might even need to confront them on aspects of their behaviour that are working against them. The mentor needs to have strong interpersonal skills to give these messages in a timely and appropriate manner. Many formal mentoring relationships never move to this stage. The mentor is often not prepared to take the risks involved in raising these issues or doesn't have the skills to convey the message. Sometimes the mentee doesn't hear the message, disagrees with the message or is unable or unwilling to change their behaviour.

Effective mentors have a high degree of expertise and knowledge in their field; the ability to exert some influence on behalf of the mentee; a genuine interest in the mentee's growth and development; a commitment to the relationship; and highly developed interpersonal skills. Mentors need to be highly skilled at listening, questioning, giving criticism, and negotiation. The mentor's key role is to assist in the development of the mentee's unique skills and abilities, not to try to clone themselves.

Role of the mentee

The term and role description for the mentee is awkward and ill-defined. This role is known by a range of terms such as the protégé, candidate, apprentice, aspirant, advisee, trainee and inductee. Each of these names carry negative associations or, as is the case with the term mentee, seem contrived. However, a more appropriate name is yet to be coined. In my early work developing mentoring programs I shortened the terms mentee and mentor to Tee and Tor. Although this began as a matter of convenience and a type of nickname, the terms as described in the Oxford Dictionary are quite appropriate; a tee being a starting place and a tor being a rocky peak or high place.

The mentee's role is to commit themselves to the mentoring program and their mentor; take on new responsibilities and challenges; seek feedback; and to accept responsibility for their own growth and development.

When selecting mentees, organisations might look for the following qualities:

- risk taking—demonstrated by, for example, a record of seeking challenging assignments and new responsibilities;
- a receptivity to feedback and coaching;
- independence—demonstrated by a history of taking responsibility for their own growth and development; and
- assessed potential to perform at one or more levels above their present position.

Program organisers need to be wary of this final point. If mentees are selected from only one form of nomination (boss), some potential mentees will be missed. Some bosses will not nominate someone for fear of losing a valuable team member to early promotion, others might be blind to someone's potential, and others are simply unwilling to see the benefits of a program that takes their team member away from their job for any time.

Benefits of mentoring programs

Structured mentoring programs are initially designed and implemented as a human resource program to assist the mentees. There are many benefits of participating in structured mentoring programs for mentees, mentors and organisations.

People entering into a mentoring relationship, as either a mentor or mentee, have an expectation that the relationship will be of some benefit to them. Whilst we traditionally think of mentoring relationships in terms of the benefits to the mentee, the mentor also expects some benefit from their input into the relationship.

Benefits to mentors

There are personal and professional benefits for mentors. Personally, mentors experience enhanced self-esteem, develop a close relationship with the mentee, fulfil their own developmental needs, receive public recognition and acclaim and can exert an extended influence on the mission and direction of the organisation. Often mentors are at a stage in their career when they begin to think about retiring or leaving an organisation. Their work with the mentee may provide for the needs of executives who want to leave a legacy to an organisation. Professionally, mentors develop a revitalised interest in their work, avoid burnout due to routine work or overload, often receive a financial reward, and obtain professional assistance on their own work projects. Laurie, a mentor in one of my programs, illustrates these points well:

> 'The recognition as someone suitable to be a mentor was encouraging and flattering.'

In many facilitated programs the mentee completes projects under the mentor's guidance and becomes an added resource for the mentor. The mentee may help the mentor to do their job, provides a source of organisational information and intelligence, and often becomes the mentor's trusted confidante. There are four key benefits for mentors: satisfaction in serving altruistically; sense of being needed; professional recognition; and increased self-esteem. Darrell, another mentor, also commented that:

> 'Working through issues and refining strategies allowed me to fine-tune some of my own techniques.'

Benefits to mentees

Mentoring programs are specifically designed to support mentees so that it follows that most books on mentoring identify many benefits to mentees. There is a recurring theme identifying the key benefits as both personal and professional gains. Mentees have support in developing and implementing targeted development activities. Mentors help mentees to avoid failure, providing an increased likelihood of success.

In the short term mentees gain specific knowledge or skills and develop an understanding of how their organisation works. The following quotes from mentees demonstrate the specific skills they anticipated gaining.

> 'The chosen project is appraisal. I expect to gain a skill in implementing appraisal structures without bulldozing people.'

> 'A new program will be in place in my school quicker than it would have been.'

There are five main benefits to mentees: access to the mentor's network; acquiring skills and knowledge; improved promotion opportunities; status; and obtaining a role model. Mentees make use of each of these benefits to varying degrees depending on the mentee, their mentor and the work situation in which mentees find themselves. Mentees also recognise different benefits of working with their partner at different stages in the relationship. Early in the relationship they see the key benefit as the acquisition of skills and knowledge. Much later in the relationship they begin to benefit from promotional opportunities. They will access the mentor's own network to varying degrees at different stages of the relationship.

Most people can identify someone they would consider to have been a mentor to them. As a child this might have been a parent or close family friend; later it might have been a particular teacher and then, if you were lucky, someone in the workplace. In the past, few people have had the benefits of working in a formal, structured mentoring relationship. With the increase in structured mentoring programs in education and industry more of our potential leaders will realise the benefits of these programs.

Informal mentoring relationships are of enormous benefit to the participants, but in many cases they rely on good luck or serendipity to form in the first place. Structured mentoring programs remove the chance factor from the establishment of the relationship. Several mentees have commented in program evaluations on how their mentoring program assisted in the development of their relationship with their mentor.

> *'It gave it a formal process. It set limits to the relationship. It made us get away from the pressures. It set up a process of how to help each other. We were determined to get everything out of it. It was a good starting point and provided a bond.'*

> *'It has set up a formal trust and confirmed our commitment.'*

> *'The program provided a structure to the relationship which would not have occurred without the program.'*

One mentee, Bob, made some significant comments which reflect the importance of the formal establishment of the relationship.

> *'It gave me the confidence to approach a mentor. I wouldn't have walked in the park and shared confidences. It has provided trust and sharing. The sharing session was excellent. It has set up a formal trust and confirmed our commitment. I wouldn't normally share my feelings with another fellow. He reciprocated. That wouldn't have happened without the program. It gave permission for us to have lunch. The structured program helped us to sort out the protocols. Darrell has developed into a real mentor, not just a coach.'*

Long-term benefits

The key long-term benefit of mentoring relationships is an improved overall performance. Mentees enhance their ability to determine their own development needs, identify development and organisational targets and pursue a plan. Mentors provide the sounding board for this development. One mentee, Hilary, anticipated this as a major benefit at the commencement of the formal program.

'1997 was a difficult year. This program will provide someone who can act as a sounding board and offer professional advice.'

Few research projects and even fewer program evaluations track program participants beyond twelve months following the conclusion of formal programs. My own anecdotal data indicates that relationships that develop to the level of sharing professionally by the conclusion of the formal program are likely to continue beyond the formal expectations of the program and develop into the next stage of friendship beyond mentoring.

Benefits to the organisation

Organisations develop and implement structured mentoring programs as part of their human resources development strategy. They expect that there will be strong benefits to the organisation. The key benefits most organisations experience include the following.

1. Increased productivity by both partners. Both partners improve their technical skills, leadership skills and motivation. These three combined have a powerful impact.
2. Improved management and technical skills. Improvement in these areas is often the catalyst for mentoring programs yet in the end, while still important, they probably have the least impact.
3. Discovery of latent talent. Both mentees and mentors discover talents and skills of which they, and others in the organisation were unaware.
4. Challenges for rusting managers. Burnt out managers are re-motivated. With flatter structures there are less promotion opportunities, and some managers become stale or burnt out. Invariably, being asked to participate in a mentor program in itself provides motivation, and then the relationship itself stimulates reflection and growth on the part of the mentor.
5. Better recruitment and retention of skilled staff. Most staff turnover occurs in the first six months. Inappropriate selection and lack of support for the new employee are major contributors to this turnover. Providing mentors for new employees helps to dramatically reduce the time that the new person needs to become productive and ensures appropriate and timely support. It also develops an increased sense of loyalty to the organisation.
6. Improved organisational communication and understanding, particularly in large cross-functional organisations. The mentor–mentee relationship provides a two-way conduit for informal communications. Members of upper management have access to grass-roots-level thinking and behaviour and the new employee or lower level manager has the opportunity to be aware of and perhaps influence strategic company thinking and planning. Organisational values and culture are passed from one generation of managers to another.

CHAPTER TWO

How Mentoring Works

Types of Mentoring ● **Mentoring Functions** ●
Program Characteristics ● **A Formal Mentoring**
Program in a Nutshell ● **Potential Pitfalls**

'We seek not to imitate the masters, rather we seek what they sought.' Anonymous Eastern philosopher

In Chapter One I likened mentoring to constructing footbridges. Taking that analogy a little further, the mentoring program designer is like the construction engineer. The engineer needs to understand the theory behind the construction and then be able to apply unique and creative solutions to each new geographic location with its specific characteristics and requirements.

Likewise, the mentoring program designer needs to understand how the mentoring process works and then be able to design programs that meet the specific needs and characteristics of each organisation and the particular participants in each program. This chapter is about how mentoring processes work.

Types of mentoring

The following types of mentoring programs can meet organisational and employee needs.

One-to-one

Traditionally one mentor works with one mentee in a close one-to-one hierarchical relationship. The mentor is at least one, if not several, levels more senior than the mentee. In present times, when organisations have flatter structures, there are fewer senior managers and those that are left have increased workloads, leaving them less time for tasks such as mentoring. There is a place for the one-to-one hierarchical mentoring model but it does reduce the pool of prospective mentors. The one-to-one mentoring model is expen-

17

sive on time and severely limits the number of matchings that can be made. It does provide a guaranteed commitment of the mentor to each mentee.

Mentoring hubs

The traditional one-to-one relationship has been redefined to include a mentor working with a number of mentees at once. On some occasions the mentor works with each mentee individually and on other occasions with all of the mentees as a group. This allows and encourages the mentees to peer coach each other and develop the 'significant peer' relationships discussed in Chapter One. This model increases the number of matchings that can be made but requires a large time commitment on the part of the mentor. It is very difficult to guarantee equal commitment to each mentee. The mentees in this type of matching will need to be more self-reliant and take more responsibility for their own development.

On-site mentors

Most organisations have only one work-site. Mentors chosen from the same work-site are easily available for ad-hoc meetings, informal shadowing and counselling. It might be difficult to identify an appropriate mentor who is more senior than the mentee but not the mentee's immediate superior. The mentor is usually considered to be someone in a more senior position than the mentee but this is not mandatory. Effective mentors can also be more experienced peers.

Off-site mentors

Larger organisations have the ability to locate mentors from a variety of work-sites. The mentee has an opportunity to see a variety of ways of working and management styles. The mentor is separate from the mentee's direct line manager. The mentoring function must be organised and formal, removing many of the opportunities for informal ad-hoc coaching and counselling. Smaller organisations with only one work-site can still consider off-site mentoring matchings by working in a co-operative arrangement with other businesses. These might be businesses in the same or related fields or they might be businesses completely different to their own. Management and leadership skills can be transferred from one setting to many others.

Decide whether your organisational and individual mentee needs will be best met by a senior mentor or a more experienced peer.

Mentoring functions

As discussed in Chapter One, mentors will be expected to motivate, support, teach, counsel, promote and protect their mentees. Depending on the mentee target group, each of these roles will take on a different significance. In the first twelve months of any mentoring relationship the mentors will be mainly motivating, coaching, supporting and counselling.

Later in the relationship they will promote and protect the mentees. These later two functions will not occur until the mentor has confidence in the mentee's abilities, believes that they are ready to take on more challenging assignments and is prepared to put their own reputation on the line to support the mentee. This level of mentoring cannot be guaranteed and relies on the personal relationship developed between the two.

Initially the mentoring relationship needs to be set in a context so that a high level of trust can develop. Two options are to base the early mentoring tasks around either a coaching or a shadowing setting. Other options for later use are given in Chapter Three.

Coaching

The mentor as coach helps the mentee to gain new skills, experiences and possibly attitudes. They provide one-to-one support and assistance through modelling, teaching and counselling. The mentee firstly identifies their current skill levels and the areas that they wish to target for development. The mentee might observe the mentor modelling these skills, work with the mentor to identify strategies that will help them to develop these skills, trial these new skills in their own workplace and finally have the mentor observe them and provide critical feedback on their performance. In some cases the mentor might not be able to provide specific coaching experiences. The role of the mentor here is to assist the mentee to identify other suitable coaches. The mentor maintains their key counselling role throughout.

The coaching model provides quite a degree of flexibility for both parties. Coaching initially demands less of the mentor. It is far less intense. This model of mentoring is most appropriate when the mentor and mentee need to maintain their regular work commitments and the mentoring function is an extra duty to be fitted in around normal daily and weekly tasks. The relationship will take longer to develop than in the shadowing model, although this is not an issue when the partners already know each other.

Shadowing

A shadow, as the name implies, is someone who follows another about as they go about their normal work. The shadow obtains an authentic understanding of their mentor's skills, behaviours and attitudes.

The purpose of the shadowing is for the mentee to observe their mentor's work, in order to learn (and perhaps provide feedback to the mentor) but not to make judgements. Shadowing is an important way of responding to the fact that in many cases highly skilled practitioners are unable to reflect on their performance. They don't know why they are good at what they do. Their skill lies in their ability to perform well, rather than their ability to reflect on and talk about their performance.

Shadowing is a way for others to observe a skilled operator performing in the workplace, with all of its constraints and unpredictablility. The experience is made more powerful if the shadowing is followed by a feedback session and discussions on what worked/didn't work and why, how things could have been handled differently, and so on.

The mentee spends an extended period of time at the mentor's worksite, observing them performing their normal duties. Each day the pair spends time discussing specific incidents. They might discuss the way that the mentor handled the situation, the background to the situation, what else has been tried, or could be tried, why the mentor acted as they did, and likely outcomes to the situation.

Prior to the shadowing exercise it is useful if the pair have discussed their preferred learning and leadership styles and identified specific skills and experiences that the mentee needs to gain. Activities that will assist the pair to identify these aspects are included in Chapter Five. Chapter Six contains a sample outline for recording shadowing observations.

The shadowing process is expensive on time. The mentee needs to be released from their normal duties for an extended period, and the mentor will only achieve a fraction of their normal workload, as the discussions around daily events take much time.

The value of the shadowing process lies in its genuineness. The observations are authentic. It is impossible to put on a show for the mentee over an extended period of time. The mentor is under quite a lot of pressure during the observation. Their mentee is watching, analysing and questioning everything they do. The relationship does develop rapidly. Both parties quickly gain an insight into their partner's real modus operandi, warts and all. The mentee gains a genuine perspective of the leadership role, usually gaining enormous respect for their mentor.

There are three rules for a mentee to follow in any shadowing exercise.

1. Be unobtrusive and do not interfere.
    It is important that the observations focus on normal work activity, not atypical one-off behaviours. The shadower should remain as unobtrusive as possible and resist the temptation to become involved, contribute, comment or even ask questions. Subsequent discussions will provide an opportunity to talk about issues and clarify what happened and why.
2. Maintain confidentiality.
    For the whole exercise to succeed a very high level of trust is required. Everything that you see or hear remains confidential. Remember that, given a second chance, we would all do some things differently. Do not be critical or judgemental. While your mentor is considered to be an expert, no-one is perfect.
3. Have follow-up discussions.
    The most valuable learning will occur in the discussion phase. Ask your mentor questions. Why did you take a particular course of action? What will you do next? What would you do differently? How do you feel about what occurred? What skills, behaviours and attitudes were used in this incident/during this time?

Program characteristics

Structured mentoring programs are all different. Each program has variations and unique characteristics. However, all programs must develop a training or support program; define the term mentor; attribute a name to the partner role; define the participants' roles; select and match participants; allow time for the relationship to develop; and evaluate the program.

While the length of the formal mentoring program can vary greatly, each program typically include three phases: pre-program; orientation and training; and relationship development. In the pre-program phase, the goals of the program are decided, participants identified, and matching takes place. An orientation or training phase follows. During this phase mentors and mentees are trained, either together or separately, on their roles and responsibilities, and a focus is set for the relationship: the mentor and mentee should establish a set of guiding principles for their relationship. The relationship then develops over a period of time that can vary greatly in length. This relationship development phase is often focused around a major project.

A formal mentoring program in a nutshell

1. Assess organisational readiness
   1.1 Assess current attitudes to training and professional development
   1.2 Assess the organisation's understanding of the concept of mentoring
   1.3 Agree on purpose, target group and mentoring options
   1.4 Define terms
2. Establish program goals
3. Pre-program phase
   3.1 Promote program
   3.2 Call for expressions of interest
   3.3 Select participants
   3.4 Match partners
   3.5 Design orientation and training program
4. Orientation and training
   4.1 Establish a rapport between partners
   4.2 Clearly articulate roles and responsibilities
   4.3 Establish protocols
   4.4 Provide skills training
   4.5 Provide a framework for the personal development plan
5. Evaluate
6. Relationship development
   6.1 Provide ongoing support
   6.2 Establish a periodic reporting program
   6.3 Facilitate meetings of all mentors

  6.4   Facilitate meetings of all mentees
  6.5   Facilitate meetings of pairs
7.   Evaluate
8.   Formal conclusion to the program

ORGANISATIONAL READINESS

Structured mentoring relationships will only be successful if the organisation understands the mentoring process and is committed to the concept of long-term professional growth. The organisation needs to allow the participants to take responsibility for their own growth and development. In particular, the organisation needs to be prepared to allow some choice in the final matching of partners, provide initial training and ongoing support for the partners, allow the partners to establish the purpose and outcome of their re- lationship, and allow time for the relationship to develop. Most importantly, the intended benefits to the individual must take precedence over the benefits to the organisation.

   The following questions can be used in discussions to assess the organisation's culture, and understanding and commitment to mentoring.

Current attitudes to training and professional development
- What currently exists to support staff growth and development?
- How does mentoring fit into other staff development initiatives?
- What are the current programs for induction of new staff, training for aspiring man- agers, support for new leaders and motivating experienced leaders?

Understanding the concept of mentoring
- What do you mean by the term mentor?
- What are the potential benefits for mentors?
- What are the potential benefits for mentees?
- What qualities should a mentor possess?
- What qualities should the mentees possess?
- Who will select the mentors?
- Who will match mentors and mentees?
- What do you see as the advantages and disadvantages of the program?

PROGRAM GOALS
- What do you hope that this program will achieve?
- How are these goals currently being met?
- Who will set the goals of the mentor program?
- Who will determine if these goals have been met?

- Who will determine the measurable outcomes for participants?
- What training will be offered to participants?
- What ongoing support will be provided?
- Who will act as sponsors of the program?
- How will the program be evaluated?

These are useful questions to be asked at a number of levels. Managers who decide to implement a mentoring program could use the questions as a reflective tool to ask themselves prior to launching into organising their own mentoring program; the human resource manager might use the questions to stimulate debate within the organisation on mentoring; the external consultant contracted to develop and/or facilitate the training for a mentoring program might use these questions as a basis for discussion. The questions will help the person responsible for establishing the program to define the organisation's current attitude to training and professional development, their understanding of mentoring, and their expectations of the program and participants.

Many organisations outsource non-core business. The development, facilitation and evaluation of professional development programs are frequently managed by consultants. The use of external consultants has some powerful advantages and a few disadvantages. The external consultant is totally committed to the success of the program, has no allegiance to any interest group, and is seen by the participants as non-partisan. They are selected on the strength of their knowledge of mentoring processes and because they are an expert training facilitator. When specialist programs such as mentoring are developed, and more importantly, facilitated by the organisation's employees, these employees are not usually experts in mentoring processes or experienced in facilitating sophisticated training programs. The external consultant, however, is a recognised expert who is committed to that particular program and has the time needed to develop, facilitate and provide on-going support.

There are also some advantages to using someone from within the organisation to facilitate the program. In larger organisations the internal program facilitator can act as a type of mentor to the mentors. This role is frequently taken on by a mentor from a previous program. They know the psychological peaks and troughs of mentoring and the peculiarities of their own particular organisation. They also have a strong commitment to the organisation. The program design and training can also be performed by someone from within the organisation but only if the organisation employs enough people to have someone on site with the knowledge of mentoring, program design expertise and training skills. Most organisations these days concentrate on their core business and outsource training and development.

It is particularly important for the external consultant to seek answers to these issues prior to beginning the assignment. Mentoring is not a 'quick fix' way of addressing skill gaps in staff expertise; it is not a guaranteed way of motivating disenchanted staff. There are no guarantees that all of the relationships will work. The benefits, as discussed in Chapter One, are real and potentially very powerful; but they are long term.

THE PRE-PROGRAM PHASE

Promote program

The promotion of the program needs to occur formally and informally. The first time that a mentoring program is conducted the promotion will be structured and rely heavily on formal processes such as articles on mentoring and in-house journals, promotional fliers and program endorsement by the CEO forwarded to all managers. In subsequent years the program should be promoted by the successful participants through the above formal processes but also by the most powerful recommendation of all—word of mouth. Participants should be encouraged or even expected to present the successful outcomes of their participation in the program in a range of forums. These forums could include, for example, speaking at the Induction Program to all new recruits, suggesting to other managers that they become mentors and nominating suitable mentees for accelerated promotion through mentoring. In fact, just talking up the program whenever they have a chance.

Call for expressions of interest

Many programs will call for expressions of interest. Your expression of interest form needs to take into account the selection and matching processes that you will be using. The form should be sent to all eligible applicants or widely advertised, asking eligible applicants to request a form. Proformas are provided in Chapter Six.

Participant selection procedures

The selection process can have a considerable impact on the success of the mentoring program and the likelihood of change and development for the mentee. Mentoring program designers need to consider issues of attracting, selecting and briefing prospective mentors. Successful programs rely on the appropriate selection of suitable mentors and mentees. The primary consideration for selection of mentees should be that they are motivated to develop different or greater competencies through an intensive relationship with their mentor.

Organisations can use a number of procedures to select participants in mentoring programs. Organisations can:
- call for volunteer mentees and mentors and accept all applicants;
- call for volunteer mentors and mentees and select suitable applicants;
- call for boss and sponsor nominations; or
- provide mentors for a group within the workplace, for example, all new employees.

Each of these options has advantages and disadvantages. If you call for volunteers and accept all applicants you will have a genuine commitment from all participants. The selection is open-ended and will encourage people prepared to take responsibility for their own professional development to apply. However, the organisation will not be able to select mentors who they believe model their corporate values, nor will the organisation be able to select mentees who they see as having potential for accelerated career development.

If organisations call for volunteer mentors and allow mentees to select from these people, there will be a commitment by these mentors, organisations do then have the ability to approve the list of mentors, and the mentees still have an element of choice in their partner. There are some disadvantages though. The mentors do not know who they are volunteering to work with; this would discourage many potential mentors from volunteering. There might not be any mentor on the list that a mentee feels comfortable with or perhaps even knows. If the mentee opts to work with an unknown mentor the relationship will take much longer to develop and is more likely to fail.

When the organisation asks for boss and sponsor nomination the potential of both mentors and mentees is being recognised and supported. The organisation can approve mentors and provide a structure with the potential to accelerate the career development of the mentees. This method involves management in the process, but it is open to accusations of nepotism or favouritism. There might not be a strong commitment to the program. Participants, once nominated by their boss or other sponsor from within the organisation, are unlikely decline the offer of participation. The pairs might not relate to each other or even know each other. Potential participants may well be missed, as people who already have high profiles are likely to be nominated.

Providing mentors for an entire group within the organisation means that anyone who could benefit from the program will have access to it. What people gain from the program really depends on what they put into it but there might not be a genuine commitment to the program and there might not be enough suitable and willing mentors.

Before selecting the mentor, program designers need to answer the following questions.

- What is the mentor's role?
- How will mentors be recruited?
- What basic characteristics should mentors possess?
- How will the mentors be rewarded?
- What support will be offered to the mentors?
- What process will be used to screen mentors?
- Will mentors self nominate or will they be recruited?
- Will participants volunteer as self-nominated pairs or individuals for the organisation to match?

The person chosen as a mentor should be a good motivator and teacher, a high performer, unthreatened by others' success, and reflect the organisation's values and culture. The most effective mentors may be those who are willing to spend the time necessary to transfer skills and knowledge and who are open enough to take risks, willing to share experience and have a desire to help.

The key aspects in selecting mentors are their commitment to the program and willingness to allocate sufficient time to the mentoring process; their ability to see the mentoring relationship as mutually beneficial; and their interpersonal skills. Mentoring is a complex and demanding job. Being mentored requires enormous risk taking. The key aspect in selecting mentees is their commitment to the program and preparedness to accept responsibility for their own growth and development.

The selection process is closely linked to the matching process and should not be seen separately.

Matching mentors and mentees

The matching of mentors and mentees in formal mentoring programs is an unpredictable process. Some partnerships will work well; others will be less successful. Informal mentoring matchings are less problematic because they occur at the instigation of the mentor, mentee or by serendipity. Despite attempts to ensure successful matchings, success in formal mentoring program matchings still hinges more on serendipity than on design. Program designers and program sponsors must keep this in mind when evaluating the success of mentoring programs.

In the case of formal mentoring programs the most effective are those in which the partners are allowed to choose each other. Where there is a degree of freedom there is a much higher success rate.

Those responsible for the matching process can:
- develop a pool of mentors from which the mentees select;
- allow mentees to self nominate with a list of their preferred mentors;
- allow mentees and mentors to apply as pairs with either partner initiating the pairing;
- match mentees and mentors who apply separately;
- call for sponsor nomination of suitable mentecs and mentors; or
- call for boss nomination of suitable mentors and mentees.

Mentees should be given the opportunity to express their choice of preferences. Mentors may then accept or reject the mentee. When the mentor chooses the mentee the mentor usually controls the development of the relationship. The mentee often takes a passive role. They rely on the experience, status, commitment, competence and energy of the mentor to provide the learning. Relationships are more likely to succeed where there is a high degree of choice, with the mentee nominating their preferred mentor and the mentor having right of refusal.

In most formal mentoring programs the organisation plays some role in the final selection of the mentees. Unsuccessful applicants might have negative reactions to the successful mentees and the organisation in general. Favouritism is a frequently heard complaint. Program designers should ensure that the criteria for selection and matching participants is clear; there are other routes for advancement and professional development; and counselling of unsuccessful applicants occurs.

Mentors and mentees look for different skills and expertise from their partners as the relationship progresses. Throughout the relationship mentors need to have highly developed interpersonal skills, demonstrate a commitment to the relationship and have specific organisational and job-related expertise as valued by the mentee. It is important to note that it is the perceptions of the mentee about the skills and expertise of the mentor that are important, not the perceptions of the organisation. Some organisations hope that they can use the mentoring program to improve an employee's knowledge, expertise or style by matching them with someone in the organisation that they believe has this knowledge, expertise or style. It is a waste of time unless the mentee also believes that their partner has something to offer them.

Similarly mentees might select their own mentor and have confidence in their skills even though the organisation does not share this confidence in the mentor's skills. Management should only interfere when they believe that the mentor is not modelling the organisation's values. Mentees do need to recognise though that when their chosen mentor is not held in high regard by their organisation they will be less able to exert any influence on their mentee's behalf. The mentor's ability to sponsor and promote the mentee will be limited.

THE ORIENTATION AND TRAINING PHASE

All participants in mentoring programs need, and appreciate, training. Orientation and training is critical to the success of the program. The purpose of the orientation and training is to provide all participants with a clear understanding of the purpose of the program and the organisation's expectations of each person's role and responsibilities; have consistent implementation of the program; have agreed and documented protocols; and to provide appropriate skill training. Detailed activities to help achieve each of these purposes are included in Chapter Five.

Establish rapport

Unless self-nominated as pairs, most mentoring pairs will not know each other very well and in some cases they might not know each other at all. The training program needs to provide opportunities for the pairs to get to know their partner. Program designers often provide one opportunity at the beginning of the formal mentoring relationship through a formal launch to the program at a dinner or drinks and nibbles, often with a guest speaker. Build from activities that are non-threatening and sharing to activities that require greater risk taking and disclosure for each party.

Roles and responsibilities

The training facilitator should outline the organisation's definitions of each role and outline what is expected of mentors and mentees and the expected outcomes of the program. Whilst this should have been clearly stated in all promotional literature and agreed to by prospective participants prior to participation in the program, it is still wise for these expectations to be clearly and publicly stated to all of the participants in one room together.

Establish protocols

It is advisable that the training facilitator outlines the aspects of the program that need to be agreed and the parameters within which the participants can set their own protocols. The protocols should include confidentiality; duration of the relationship; meetings; roles and responsibilities of the mentee and mentor; the approximate time to be invested by the mentor; and how to terminate an unsuccessful relationship prior to the formal conclusion of the program.

The organisation will have established the non-negotiable aspects of these protocols. These will usually include conditions such as the minimum number of meetings; the duration of the formal relationship; the use of specific tools such as competency profiles as the basis of the personal development plan; and the relationship of the mentor to the mentee's boss.

Each pair should then agree on the protocols for their relationship. This will include aspects such as the location of meetings, length of time, approximate number of meetings, who can initiate meetings, and what will be discussed, and each person's specific expectations of their partner.

Not all relationships will be successful. In some cases it will be necessary to terminate the formal mentoring relationship prior to the conclusion of the program. It is important that either the mentor or mentee can initiate this process with no negative consequences. Program facilitators will usually seek feedback from both people as to the cause of the breakdown in the relationship, however their purpose is to avoid future unsuccessful matchings rather than to lay blame with the participants.

Provide appropriate skill training

It is assumed that the mentors will have been selected because of their acknowledged expertise in their chosen field. If the mentor does not already have highly developed inter-personal skills before selection to the program, skills training in this area is unlikely to provide the mentor with the necessary level of competence in this area. The training program should provide mentors with refresher training in this area and focus on developing their role with the mentee. Mentees need skill development in negotiation, listening, and questioning. The mentors and mentees need skill development in goal setting, planning, negotiation, communication and giving criticism.

A full day of orientation and training for the mentees, with the mentors joining in the second half of the day, is a good option. Mentors are usually senior people within organisations and will often begrudge a full day commitment.

Provide the framework for a personal development plan

The purpose of the relationship is to develop the mentee's skills and abilities. The mentor and mentee need to establish what skills and abilities the mentee should possess and identify existing strengths and weaknesses.

The mentee can use a number of tools to conduct a skills audit. There are a number of management competency profiles available. It is useful for the mentee to seek feedback on their skill levels from a range of other people. The mentee can use the competency profile to seek feedback from their manager, one or two work peers and one or two people who report to them. This process is known as seeking a 360° view. It provides valuable insights into the mentee's skills, as perceived by a range of other people in the work context.

The feedback provided in the competency profiles is then used as the basis for discussions with the mentor when formulating the mentee's personal development plan. The profiles will confirm the mentee's perceptions of their strengths and development areas and challenge some perceptions, as well as reveal blind spots that could be strengths or weaknesses.

THE RELATIONSHIP DEVELOPMENT PHASE

The success of formal mentoring programs depends on the strength of the relationship that develops between the partners. In some cases this relationship will develop naturally and quickly move from reticence to open disclosure. This is unusual. Program designers cannot leave the relationship development to chance. Activities that promote openness and disclosure need to be built into the orientation program and followed up in the mid-cycle training. The formal program should provide structures that require the partners to work together on high-level tasks for extended periods of time.

The participants will move between the various stages in the relationship at their own rate. The stages should be seen as a continuum rather than steps. Unfortunately but predictably, some partners will move quickly to the break-up stage, other partners will remain stationary at a particular point on the continuum. The relationship is more likely to develop when the partners work together for longer periods of time on more demanding tasks that develop a high degree of trust between the partners.

Provide on-going support

The relationship development phase is the key to the success of any formal program. Each pair will go through the normal ups and down of any close relationship. It useful to have a person whose role it is to provide support to mentors and mentees in each pair at the critical points in the relationship. The support person should not be in a line management relationship with any of the participants. They might be the training facilitator, a previous mentor, or experienced human resource facilitator within or outside the organisation. It does not need to be the same person for all pairs. Support could be provided from a team with each pair having their own support person. This person does need to have highly developed interpersonal communication skills in listening, questioning, negotiating and conflict resolution.

The support person provides personal support for the mentor and mentee; ensures that clear goals for the relationship are established; provides motivation and an informal degree of accountability that pairs are meeting and that the relationship is on track; and may act as a mediator.

Regardless of the selection and matching process there will be some pairs that just don't jell. The support person might be needed to resolve conflicts over perceived roles and expectations, misunderstandings with the mentee's manager, or personality clashes. In some cases the support person might need to suggest that the formal mentoring relationship is terminated. Each partner needs to accept that this might be the resolution to the situation. Fault should not be allocated in this situation. The support person should try to establish why the relationship broke down simply to avoid other potentially unsuccessful matchings. Participants must be clear that the no fault divorce means exactly that and that there will be no negative consequences to them dropping out of the program.

Establish a periodic reporting program

In all programs some matchings will be highly successful and require very little support, however, most relationships will fluctuate. Immediately following the orientation and training pairs will be highly motivated. The critical point is approximately four to six weeks after the initial training. It is important that the support person contacts each person in the program to evaluate if the pairs have been meeting, the participants' perceptions of the value of these meetings, and to identify any potential sources of conflict.

These telephone calls invariably prompt those pairs that have not been meeting to initiate contact and 'get a move on'. The support person should initially contact the participants separately rather than meeting with the pairs, as participants will be reluctant to disclose any dissatisfaction or frustration with their partner in front of them. Contact should be made by the support person with each participant approximately once every six weeks.

Participants should also be encouraged to contact the support person at any stage that they would appreciate some assistance.

Facilitate group meetings for participants

Halfway through the relationship development phase, participants enjoy the opportunity to meet to discuss how their development plan is progressing, what tools have been useful, and problems that they have encountered. The group might provide solutions to these problems or just make participants aware that they are not alone. It is useful to allow time at this stage of the program for the participants to work as like groups. The mentors and mentees enjoy time with other mentors and mentees to discuss issues pertinent to their role in the program and discuss how others are managing the role.

Participants might also need specific skill training in this session. The person providing support to each pair will have identified specific skill needs during their contact telephone calls. When this role is being performed by a number of people the training facilitator will need to co-ordinate feedback on these training needs.

EVALUATING THE PROGRAM

Mentoring relationships are complex and their success is largely serendipitous. The protocols and guidelines outlined earlier in this chapter will increase the likelihood of success but are no guarantees. Each program should be progressively evaluated at every stage. Programs appearing to be successful in the short term may be less successful if viewed in the long term and vice versa. Organisations should have clearly identified the short- and long-term goals for the mentoring program at the very beginning. These goals should then form the basis of the evaluation at each phase of the program.

Evaluations should occur following the orientation phase, each subsequent training session, at the conclusion of the formal program, and finally at the conclusion of the first, and perhaps second, year following the program. The evaluation after the orientation phase should assess the initial program advertising and promotion, selecting and matching procedures, training program and support material such as manuals and resource lists. Sample evaluation proformas are included in Chapter Six.

At the conclusion of the formal program the following aspects should be assessed: support provided by the program facilitator and the organisation; follow-up training programs; skills of the mentor; gains made by the mentee; and success of particular learning activities. The organisation will want to determine if there has been a significant change in the mentee's performance as perceived by the mentee themselves, their mentor and their line manager. Have the short-term goals been met from each person's point of view?

Long-term goals for mentoring programs could be a reduced staff turnover following induction of new staff, fast tracking staff members with leadership potential, providing leadership opportunities for staff from minority or disadvantaged groups, or providing a support structure for newly appointed leaders. The success of some mentoring relationships cannot be fairly judged immediately following the formal program.

FORMAL CONCLUSION

It is important that there is a formal conclusion to the formal mentoring relationship. Some pairs will have jelled and may choose to continue to meet as informal mentoring partners, but most pairs will cease the formal relationship at the conclusion of the program. A final session with all of the participants allows participants to share their successes with others, provides the opportunity to evaluate the program, and provides a forum for the organisation to recognise the contribution made by the participants and formally conclude the program.

This session should allow time for the pairs to privately show their appreciation to their partner, publicly acknowledge their achievements and evaluate the program to date, and for the organisation to publicly recognise the contribution of the participants through the awarding of certificates or awards.

Chapter Four contains more information on program design; Chapter Five has sample activities; Chapter Six contains useful proformas.

Potential pitfalls

Mentoring programs are undoubtedly beneficial to mentees, mentors and organisations but, as with all programs, there are some potential problems or pitfalls. With some fore-thought these can generally be overcome.

Pitfalls	Possible causes	Possible solutions
Being a fad rather than part of the organisation's professional development strategy	Not establishing the organisation's readiness	Communicate with all levels of the organisation to establish realistic expectations for the program and identify how the program links to other human resource strategies
Uncommitted mentors or mentees	Pressure from the organisation to participate	Allow voluntary participation
	Change in job expectations of either party	Renegotiate expectations if the situation changes Renegotiate partner
	Unclear expectations of participants	Clearly establish expectations prior to selection
Mentors not taking their role seriously	Poor training	Provide training in skill areas required of mentors
	Role expectations not established	Clearly establish the role expectations prior to selection
	Little reward for mentors	Reward mentors (not necessarily by remuneration) Allow no fault divorce
Mentees receiving no or poor feedback	Lack of training	Provide adequate training
	Inappropriate selection	Review selection procedures

Pitfalls	Possible causes	Possible solutions
Unrealistic expectations by mentors, mentees or the organisation	Inadequate preparation	Establish short- and long-term goals for the organisation, mentors and mentees
	Expectations not articulated in the training and manuals	Publish the organisational goals
		Program facilitator to monitor mentor and mentee expectations
	Inappropriate matching	Review matching processes
Mentor taking credit for the mentee's work	Inappropriate selection	Counsel mentee and mentor
		Review selection procedures
		Possible rematch
Mentor using mentee as extra member of staff	Misunderstanding program goals

Role expectations unclear | Clearly outline and publish program goals and role expectations |
	Poor training	Review training procedures
Managers using mentoring to prop up poor performers	Misunderstanding program goals	Discuss program goals
	Poor supervision skills	Train the manager in supervision
Unsuccessful matching	Personality clash	Review selection and matching procedures
	Difference in styles or standards	Allow a no fault divorce
	Poor selection or matching	
Discontent among non-participants	Jealousy for not being selected	Increase opportunities for appropriate matchings
	Misunderstanding of program goals	Promote program goals more widely

Pitfalls	Possible causes	Possible solutions
Mentoring not seen to be immediately achieving the agreed goals	Unrealistic expectations on the timeline	Allow sufficient time before judging the effectiveness
	Not devoting sufficient time to the mentoring role	Provide time for participants
	Not providing sufficient time to the mentoring pairs	Participants allocate sufficient time
	Compulsory participation	Allow voluntary participation
Insufficient applications to participate in the program	Inadequate advertising and promotion	Review advertising and promotion strategy
	Lack of support for participants	Program goals misunderstood
	Too many work pressures	Provide adequate resources
Time-management issues	Mentoring program placing unrealistic demands on participants	Review program expectations
	Lack of commitment	Review HR strategy and place of mentoring
	Program not an integral part of human resource strategy	
	Orientation and training program too long	

Mentoring in the Workplace

Perceptions of Learners ● **Developing Strong Mentor Relationships** ● **Role of the Facilitator in the Relationship** ● **Factors that Influence the Decline of the Relationship** ● **Behaviours that Help the Relationship to Mature**

'Have you learned lessons only from those who admired you, and were tender with you? Have you not learned great lessons from those who braced themselves against you, and disputed the passage with you?' Walt Whitman

The mentoring program is all about developing goals and a learning program for the mentee. There are many ways that the mentor can help the mentee to learn and develop.

Perceptions of Learners

Mentors may view the mentee and the learning environment in a variety of ways. Their perception of the learning process will influence the direction that the relationship takes.

The empty vessel

In this view the mentor sees the mentee as devoid of the skills, knowledge and experiences that the mentor has accumulated over the years. Their role is to transmit these competencies to the mentee. This relationship is mentor-directed and undervalues the capacity of the mentee to organise and structure their own learning.

The seed

The mentee is seen as a plant which, given the right conditions, will grow. The mentor is seen as a gardener who tends and nurtures the growing plant. This model assumes that every mentee has potential and, given time and the appropriate conditions, the mentee will reach that potential.

The patient

The mentee is seen as someone needing to be 'fixed up'. The mentor provides remedies or solutions for something that is not working. In this model the mentor is seen as the 'caregiver', responsible for the health or recovery of the mentee.

The ladder

The mentor thinks of the mentee as someone climbing a ladder. The ladder provides the one and only path to the top. Each rung on the ladder is a skill or experience that the mentee needs to climb to the next rung. In this view the mentor has already climbed the same ladder and can provide strategies for gaining the skills and ensure that the mentee has access to the necessary experiences.

The explorer

The mentee is seeking to understand and discover their own route. In this view the mentor's role is to guide and counsel, helping the mentee plan the most appropriate route for themselves and learn how to overcome obstacles along the way.

No matter how the mentor sees the learning process, the process will include the following three steps.

1. Establish the goals for the mentee.
    The mentor works with the mentee to clarify their needs and short- and long-term goals. The mentor can also work with the mentee to identify their current competencies. Specific industry-based tools, such as competency audits, or performance appraisals, might be used, or less formal processes, based around discussions with the mentor, interviews with the mentee's manager, or mentor observations of the mentee's performance, might be used.

    The partners spend some time discussing these issues to develop goals and an action plan. In some cases this initial process can be achieved in days, in other cases it might take months. The length of time will be dependent on such things as how well the pair knew each other to begin with, the personal style of the partners, the time available to achieve these tasks and previous experience in goal setting.
2. Develop an action plan to achieve the goals.
    The partners agree on the most suitable activities to meet the mentee's needs, and develop an action plan that clearly states what will occur; when; how the activities will be organised; who is responsible for organising each activity; and what are the expected outcomes of each activity.
3. Identify strategies that make best use of the knowledge, skills, experiences and personal style of the mentor and the constraints placed on both parties by their job and workplace.

Strategies that have worked for others include those listed below. Shadowing and coaching are dealt with in more detail in Chapter One.

Shadowing

The mentee follows around as an expert goes about their daily work. This expert might be the mentor or an expert in another field. The mentee observes the way the expert works and then discusses these observations to identify ways to improve their own performance.

Trialling

The mentee selects an idea or process and sets up a situation in which it can be piloted before being fully implemented.

Job rotation

The mentee rotates through different jobs every few months, gaining experience in all divisions of the organisation.

Project work

The mentee becomes part of a project team set up around one of their learning goals. This will help them to learn specific skills related to the project and to learn to work as part of a team.

Coaching

The mentee seeks out people with specific technical skills from within the organisation (internal coaches) or from outside the organisation (external coaches). The coaches must also have coaching skills and a willingness to pass on their knowledge and expertise. The mentor might play an influential role here in identifying coaches and arranging their participation in the coaching process.

Counselling

Some of the most valuable learning will occur when the mentee meets with the mentor and discusses on-the-job learning and experiences and regularly reflects on what is working well and not so well. The mentor plays a key role in encouraging the mentee to identify and resolve their own problems.

Visits off-site

The mentee looks at examples of good practice in other workplaces. This experience is then discussed with their mentor to clarify the learning and suggest improvements in their own workplace. This could lead to a workplace activity such as trialling. Key roles for the mentor are helping to identify examples of good practice and gaining entry to such places.

Research

The mentor provides ideas on professional reading and other training available through manuals, videos, CD-ROM programs, and kits. The pair spend time discussing personal learning from these and also implications for the organisation.

Developing strong mentor relationships

Another extremely important aim of all structured mentoring programs is to initiate and then support strong mentoring relationships that outlast the formal program. There are a number of processes and procedures that organisations and program facilitators can use to facilitate strong ongoing relationships. But at the end of the day the success of the program is largely determined by aspects outside the control of the organisation or the program facilitator—mainly the chemistry that develops between the mentor and the mentee. By understanding the stages that each relationship might travel through and the conditions that are likely to assist participants to move up through these levels, program designers can increase the number of on-going relationships that are likely to develop as an outcome of the program.

On occasions the relationship will be terminated. This is usually because the disadvantages of a continued relationship outweigh the advantages. In most cases longer term mentor relationships that are no longer serving the needs of one or both partners are terminated at the instigation of the mentee. This is usually because either one or both partners are having difficulty redefining the relationship from one of formal mentoring to one of peer support and friendship. This frequently happens when the mentee progresses to a similar or higher level of seniority to their mentor.

STAGES IN THE RELATIONSHIP

There are up to five stages in formal mentoring relationships. Not all relationships will go through each of these stages, nor will relationships move at the same rate through the stages. Each pair is unique. Some pairs in formal relationships stay at the formal and cautious stage, many pairs only reach the exploratory risk taking, some reach sharing professionally and only a few share personally or move beyond the mentoring relationship. The program facilitator can improve the likelihood of movement to higher levels by preparing the participants during the training for the likely stages in the relationship. If the participants understand the purpose of particular activities performed at particular times in the relationship, and understand their feelings towards their partner at certain times, they might be more willing to push the relationship to reach the next level.

1. Formal and cautious

At the beginning of the relationship the participants will be distant, respectful and possibly apprehensive. The main mentoring activities are teaching and role modelling. When working on a project with or for the mentor, the mentee will probably check most activities with the mentor. When working independently of the mentor the mentee will share superficial concerns only. Both partners need to be prepared to spend sufficient time in both social and work situations to get to know each other. Time needs to be allocated for the partners to observe each other's learning and management styles and discuss these observations with each other. There will be a lot of listening, clarifying and questioning, until both parties are confident enough for the mentee to take increased responsibility and take some professional risks in their learning.

The key ingredient at this stage is spending time observing each other and talking about these observations.

2. Exploratory risk taking

As the relationship develops the partners develop increased trust and confidence. The main mentoring activities are counselling and personal support.

The mentor working with the mentee gives the mentee greater latitude and freedom in carrying out tasks. The mentor also encourages the mentee to take greater risks in developing and implementing their own learning goals. For the new employee, the mentor imparts a feel for the job, a knowledge of the skills needed and trends in the industry. The mentor also discusses knowledge about managing people in the organisation, and gaining supporters in the organisation. In some cases, the mentor has developed sufficient confidence to allow the mentee to make independent decisions and manage projects.

In other programs where the mentee is working as a manger in their own right, the mentee will use the mentor more as a sounding board. The mentee will discuss the projects that they are working on, seeking advice and encouragement in their risk taking.

The key ingredient at this stage is the development of trust and confidence in each other. The mentor encourages the mentee through confidence building and pep talks. Structures need to be provided to encourage the developing trust and confidence in each other. The primary investments are emotion and self disclosure. Both partners need to be prepared to discuss aspects of their work that frustrate, excite, challenge, worry, stress, bore them. Respect and confidentiality are paramount. In order to move to the next level in the relationship the mentor needs to be prepared to begin to discuss their own struggles and deficiencies. Many formal mentoring relationships reach this stage but do not move to the next level.

3. Sharing professionally

Mutual understanding and trust are developing. By now the mentor has a high degree of confidence in the mentee's abilities and is beginning to use their own organisational relationships to the mentee's advantage. Both partners have developed a working knowledge of the skills and deficiencies of their partner. Both partners confide in each other about their professional struggles, goals and plans for attaining these goals. The mentor provides a sense of perspective, particularly to the mentee new to a leadership position. They can help the mentee to overcome the pressures of a new position by accentuating the positive factors and building the confidence of the mentee.

This is the highest level that an organisation can expect that a formal mentoring relationship will reach. If participants reach this stage most organisations' goals for mentoring programs will have been met. Many relationships do not reach this level as the mentor is not prepared to confide in the mentee. A high level of trust and confidence in the partner needs to have developed for pairs to reach this stage. This can take many years and most formal mentoring programs do not track pairs for that period of time. The key ingredients here are time working together, mutual respect and mutual gain from the relationship.

4. Sharing personally

As the professional sharing develops it naturally moves into personal support. The mentor will often counsel the mentee about personal life issues and long-term career goals. They might also help the mentee to manage the family and personal pressures that interfere with job performance. They may share some issues from their own personal life. Some of these activities might be performed at earlier stages in the relationship, but at this stage mutual personal sharing occurs with the mentee providing support to the mentor as well as vice versa.

Mentors might also protect the mentee from organisational conflicts and situations that might affect their advancement, promote the abilities and skills of the mentee within and beyond the organisation, and provide the mentee with access to resources and networks that would ordinarily be unavailable to the mentee.

5. Friendship beyond mentoring

Some mentor pairs will maintain the relationship beyond the formal program expectations. To do this the pair needs to be able to redefine the relationship and let go of the helper/helpee model. A genuine friendship develops and the relationship is now defined in these terms. Some of the barriers that prevent this from occurring are jealousy on the part of the mentor who might find that 'their' mentee has reached the same level of seniority as them or even beyond it, patronising attitudes of mentors, and mentees who see the mentor as a potential threat because they know the mentee 'warts and all'.

Throughout the relationship mentees are looking to their mentor to provide advice and counsel in organisational and job-related issues to help them develop interpersonal skills and to show a commitment to their relationship. The balance of these changes as the relationship develops. As it moves into a true mentoring relationship the mentor provides little job-related advice; the key requirements are their interpersonal skills and their commitment to their mentee. Early in the relationship most mentors are genuinely committed to their role as mentor but they need time to development a commitment to, and confidence in, their mentee as a person.

There is no formula that defines how long pairs will spend at each stage. However, there are some patterns. Pairs who do not know each other prior to the structured program will take at least three months to move into the risk-taking phase. This can be accelerated by increasing the amount of time spent together. Most structured programs only require the pairs to initially meet three to four times for between one and three hours over a period of three months. At this level of intensity, the relationship will take a long time to develop. Organisations and individual managers will determine how much time they are prepared to allow mentees to take from their regular work to apply to the mentor relationship. Successful pairs find time to meet over and above the prescribed time commitment. Mentor programs that demand a high initial contact time between the pairs, such as shadowing programs, accelerate movement through the stages considerably.

Many pairs find that their relationship suddenly changes following a crisis point faced by the mentee during which they sought and received genuine help from their mentor. The support generally takes the form of counselling and confidence building. Real growth takes place when the relationship has developed to a point where the pair trust each other enough to talk openly about their relationship and other professional concerns. This occurred for one mentee when her manager died suddenly at work. The mentor worked at a different work location. After hearing of the tragedy the mentor went to be with the mentee; talked with her about what needed to be done to inform appropriate people, how to counsel other employees, what to say to the family of the manager; and generally provided emotional support to the mentee. The mentor admits that had the formal mentoring program not been in place, she would not have felt that it was her role to provide this support. She also admitted that no doubt no-one else in the organisation would have stepped in as quickly. They both noticed the marked change in their relationship from that point and spoke to me about it.

The length of the risk-taking phase and the professional sharing is highly unpredictable. My own research and anecdotal evidence indicates that relationships need approximately two years of constant nurturing to move into personal sharing and beyond mentoring. Few mentoring pairs will experience an event as traumatic and bonding as the death of a colleague but many other pairs have described to me a time when they appreciated their mentor being there to provide psychological support. When this support is there over a period of time trust develops and a real friendship begins.

Activities performed at each level

The following table outlines some of the typical activities performed at each level.

	Teach	Counsel	Sponsor
Formal and cautious	Defining the job Coaching in specific skills needed to perform the job	Guidance on available career paths Correct presentation of self	Introductions to meetings and structures not normally accessed at the mentee's level
Risk taking	People management Strategies for fast tracking Technical skills	Internal politics Corporate taboos Confidence building and encouraging the mentee to take greater responsibility	Recommending the mentee for positions of responsibility Advertising the mentee's qualities and skills
Sharing	Stress management Politicking High-level communication skills	Keeping things in perspective Using networks and position Specific career counselling	Protection by intervening in situations that might threaten the mentee's progress Requiring the mentee to represent the mentor in situations normally beyond their level

At each stage of the relationship the mentor teaches, counsels and sponsors. As the relationship moves along the continuum the activities being performed by the mentor become more sophisticated. The personal nature of the support provided increases in intensity. The mentor must be prepared to confide in their mentee firstly about their own working style and strategies for managing issues such as internal politics and eventually to reveal some of their own deficiencies and strategies of managing these.

Mentoring is a demanding and complex role. It will be a tiring and emotionally draining experience. You will feel frustration, anxiety, pleasure and satisfaction. The mentoring process forces mentors and mentees to reassess their management and learning style and put their operations and shortcomings under a microscope.

Role of the facilitator in the relationship

The facilitator plays a small but pivotal role at each level. The program designer will ensure that during the initial training there are activities that develop a rapport between the partners and the program facilitator. The program design should also include activities that allow the mentees and, more importantly, the mentors to get to know each other. I have found that it is useful for the mentors in particular to form a network with other mentors. Mentors are the type of people who are always interested in broadening their own networks. It is also handy for them to have other mentors to act as reference points to bounce ideas off or use as a sounding board around issues to do with their mentoring role.

Familiarisation

During the initial training the program facilitator spends time observing the pairs, getting to know individual styles, strengths and weaknesses. It is a wise idea to take notes of the particular characteristics of individuals and pairs to jog your memory for later in the program. In many cases you never use these notes but they will come in handy when you least expect it.

Keeping partners in touch

Immediately following the orientation program pairs are highly motivated and make many plans to meet and work together. As the year progresses and other regular work pressures accumulate, the regularity of the meetings drops off. It is at this point that the program facilitator must act. A quick telephone call to each participant six to twelve weeks after the orientation training is a useful prompt. Commitment is sometimes waning at this point. Guilt can be useful.

The timely phone call might be all that is needed to motivate the pair to meet again or keep to original plans. This phone call can also be used to ascertain if the relationship is working but needs a boost or if there are problems that need addressing. I have used this technique in all of the programs that I have facilitated. For one program this was an essential strategy that had an enormous impact on one relationship. In the routine telephone call to the mentor (Pam) I noted that the mentee (Hilary) had not kept any of the last three appointments (the first two were cancelled and the third simply forgotten). I next contacted Hilary, to find that she was under a lot of stress and felt overwhelmed by her new management role. I had noted in the orientation training that Hilary was concerned about the difference between Pam's style and her own.

Pam could be very abrupt and gave the impression of being highly efficient and organised. She was a logical thinker and decision maker. Emotion and intuition played little part. Pam was seen to be a 'shaker and mover' who definitely got things done. Her listening and other interpersonal skills were adequate but not a strength. Hilary was quiet, lacked confidence, but a creative, unusual thinker. Hilary had requested Pam as her mentor because she felt that Pam had a toughness that would benefit her in her new role as a manager.

I was concerned about both Hilary and the problems that had developed in the relationship. I rang Pam again suggesting that she drop into Hilary's workplace on the pretext of being in the area and catching a quick coffee. I mentioned some of my concerns to Pam but only briefly. Pam's impromptu visit lasted three hours and led to major changes in Hilary's practice and her relationship with Pam. In a later conversation with Hilary she commented to me about the sudden change in Pam's attitude and style. (Hilary never knew of my intervention.) Pam was suddenly seen to be interested and genuinely committed to Hilary's welfare.

For Bill and Trevor, a pair in another program, my contact call had similar positive results. In contact conversations that I had with Bill (the mentor), he said that he was feeling a little frustrated because he and his mentee seemed to have lost direction and were just ambling along. Following our discussions he decided to invite Trevor (his mentee) out for a meal and to discuss his concerns directly with his partner. At this time they both shared their frustration. Trevor's work tasks had changed since the beginning of the program and it was a timely exercise for him. Bill used his network to help Trevor access some short-term coaching, and Bill took on a role of encouraging Trevor and providing psychological support and confidence building. They increased their contact but were generally using quick telephone calls or snatched meetings so that the amount of time they spent did not change greatly.

A second benefit of the telephone calls is to determine the training needs of the partners for the mid-cycle training program. During your conversations with each partner note their concerns, common issues being raised and aspects of leadership or management that mentees have focused through their individual development plans. You will need to hone your listening and questioning skills.

Terminating

Unfortunately, there will be some occasions during these contacts when the facilitator will pick up that the relationship needs to be terminated. It is important to stress to both parties there will be no stigma attached to enacting a no fault divorce. If either party finds that the disadvantages of continuing the relationship outweigh the advantages, allow them to part.

Future program facilitators will find it helpful if you can determine the cause of the relationship breakdown but, as in all relationships, it will be difficult to agree on what exactly went wrong. Once you have all agreed that there is no gain in continuing the relationship as mentor and mentee, formally agree with both partners that they have no further commitments to each other or the program. Follow this up in writing with a note of appreciation for their contributions (even if minimal). This might encourage them to participate in future programs.

Factors that influence the decline of the relationship

Most of the unsuccessful mentoring relationships end 'not with a bang but a whimper'. The most common cause is the lack of time being invested by one or both of the partners. This can be caused by work overload, distance or a number of other factors outside the control of the other parties. Partners who fail to develop a rapport or mutual respect for their partner's skills and abilities are the ones most likely to melt into the distance. Some relationships break down when the mentee decides that their mentor is either unwilling or unable to deliver on the promised or expected expertise.

Some relationships fail following a breakdown in trust such as one partner breaching issues of confidentiality. Tension within the relationship also develops when there is a difference in expectations. The likelihood of this occurring is reduced by raising these issues in the orientation program but, no matter how often or how clearly these expectations are stated, there will be occasions when one member of a pair believes that their partner's requests are unrealistic.

Fortunately, most relationships follow a more productive path. While they may not all end in lifelong friendship, most mentees receive valuable professional support, guidance and expert advice from their mentor.

Behaviours that help the relationship to mature

Behaviours of mentors

As said before, listening, questioning and the ability to ascertain the strengths and weaknesses of the mentee are key interpersonal skills. One mentee believed that a good mentor had the:

> 'ability to work with you in a non-threatening way ... a critical
> friend, questioning what and why I do things and offering strat-
> egies I had not thought of. Providing another way of doing things.'

Mentors will also need to demonstrate a commitment to the relationship. This will occur in different ways depending on the individuals. In many cases the mentor will need to initiate early meetings. Mentees are often reluctant to 'bother' the mentor who might seem to be so much more important than them. The mentor might need to initiate some of the first meetings and seem to lead these meetings but it is important that the mentor shares the decision making about the relationship with their partner. Issues such as the location and timing of meetings needs to be agreed and shared. Meetings, for example, should take place at both of their workplaces and not always at one. It will be up to the mentor to encourage the mentee to take an increasing responsibility for the development of the relationship, but the initial nurturing usually needs to come from the mentor.

The focus of their interpersonal skills changes during the relationship. They also need to build up the mentee's confidence and encourage them to take greater risks in their learning. Learning can be challenging and exciting but it can also be a little threatening. When we try new ways of operating we usually feel uncomfortable and insecure. It is at this point that the mentor can really make an impact. The mentor needs to encourage their partner to persevere with the new ideas/strategies until they become skilled in their use and not to fall back on old ways.

When we try a new approach to tackling an old problem our level of competence drops, sometimes well below our previous level. This often happens when we get some coaching in sport. We've been hitting the golf ball with a particular swing for years and doing OK—not brilliant but OK. With a bit of coaching we should be brilliant. After the coaching we find that we have actually regressed. Scores are worse. A good coach keeps up our motivation to persevere with the new technique so that before too long our skill level far outpaces our original standard. It is at the interim skill level that the motivational coaching is imperative. After we have tried the new technique for a while and found that our skill levels are not improving—in fact they are getting worse—we need cajoling and motivation to keep at it. In the mentoring role the mentor can help to motivate their partner when their skill levels drop and seem to be plateauing at an even lower level than before they tried the new technique.

It is a balancing act between pushing, letting go and supporting. The critical quality that the mentor needs though is a genuine commitment to their partner, which is demonstrated by their willingness and availability during crisis times as well as providing support through the original planned strategy.

The following comments made to me by two different mentees highlight this well.

> '[The mentors] need to be available and flexible. The mentor will have a willingness to communicate over a period of time, availability and flexibility. A willingness to provide time in varying degrees—at times close contact over a few days and at other times a phone call or little contact. The ability to put up with you hassling them.'

> 'If I'm having a bad day I ring and say I need coffee now. We drop whatever we are doing to offer support.'

I should stress though that the mentor is not permanently 'on call'. Relationships are based on give and take. The mentor needs to be available and flexible, as noted by our first mentee, but only asked to 'drop everything' for the genuine crisis. When describing the turning point in her relationship with her mentor one mentee talked of the time she faxed a note of despair to her mentor at the end of a particularly stressful day. Within an hour a return fax arrived of an appropriate cartoon. This was followed up the next day with a phone call, by which stage the mentee had had a night's sleep and was coping again. The mentor had completely forgotten the incident but the mentee describes it as a turning point for her. She believed that the mentor was there providing psychological support and had confidence that the mentee would resolve the issues herself.

Behaviours of mentees

Successful relationships of all types are based on the contributions of both partners, and mentoring relationships are no different. Initially, like mentors, mentees also need interpersonal skills and to show a commitment to the relationship but these skills and the way they demonstrate their commitment is different.

Mentees also need a flexibility of approach. The mentee needs to have the ability and willingness to look at issues from different points of view and to try many approaches to problem identification and problem solving.

Mentees need to view their mistakes as a learning experience. They need to have a commitment to their own professional development which they see as a life-long process. This an important characteristic that will be considered in the selection process for the mentees but for many mentees it will be something they had given little conscious thought to. It is also an attitude that can be developed and nurtured by mentors. For open-minded mentees with a flexible approach to their work this will not be hard.

At the beginning of the relationship they will have some commitment to the program but this is dependent on their belief in what the mentor 'can do for them'. They need to develop a commitment to their partner and be prepared to share in the work and time involved in developing a sense of trust in each other. The mentee needs to be able to identify their own needs or be willing to expose themselves to their mentor so that together they can discover the mentee's development needs.

Program Design

Training Support ● Orientation ● Mid-Cycle ● Relationship Closure ● Final Recommendations

By now you will have an appreciation of the benefits of mentoring programs. You have spent some time developing an understanding of how to develop the strongest and most appropriate framework for your mentoring program. The success of the program now hinges on the quality of the training and support program provided by the organisation. This chapter provides practical and fun activities to develop mentors' and mentees' skills at each stage of the relationship.

Remember the construction engineer? You have now studied the theory of bridge construction and applied the theory to your particular requirements. You are now ready to design and build your own unique bridge.

This table is useful at the design stage of your mentoring program. Agree on the key purpose of your program. Identify the target group of mentees. Determine the resources that the organisation is prepared and able to put into the mentoring program; the organisational restrictions placed on the program design; and the needs of the mentors and mentees.

Purpose	Target group	Mentoring options
Induction	New staff	Coaching
Succession planning	New leaders	Shadowing
Supporting isolated employees	Potential leaders	1:1
Reducing burn-out	Minority groups	1:many
Supporting the organisational philosophy	Under-represented groups	On-site mentor
	Isolated employees	Off-site mentor
	High fliers	More senior mentor
	Experienced leaders	More experienced peer mentor
Choose one of the above	Choose one of the above	Choose combinations from above

Training Support

In formal mentoring programs training should occur in the orientation stage, mid-cycle and at the conclusion of the formal relationship. The specific content of each of these sessions will be decided by the program facilitator, depending on the particular needs of the participants.

The following is an overview of the possible training goals for each stage. Specific training activities are discussed in detail in Chapter Five.

Orientation

Well-structured orientation activities will help to ensure the success of the program. Orientation should take one half to one full day. If there are strong time pressures on mentors, involve them for the half day only.

Orientation should include activities that:
- demonstrate a high level of commitment by management;
- establish organisational goals;
- establish non-negotiable roles and responsibilities;
- outline best practice for mentoring relationships;
- provide skill training for mentors and mentees;
- develop a rapport between partners;
- identify personal working styles;
- appraise current performance or competency;
- establish expectations and protocols for all stakeholders;
- provide strategies for goal setting, action planning and tracking progress; and
- give participants exposure to others' experiences and evaluate the program so far.

Commitment of management

The kudos given to the program can have a significant impact on the attitude of the participants, the mentees' line managers, those not selected for the program and the next group of prospective applicants. The manner in which the program is launched can influence the attitudes of each of these stakeholders and so have an impact on the success of the program. Organise an official launch. This can occur at the conclusion of the initial orientation training or at a social gathering of participants prior to the training.

Launch the program with the most senior member of the organisation's management team that you can gain access to. Arrange publicity. Organise photographs to be taken. Interview new mentor pairs and previous mentor pairs if there are any. Recognise the contribution of participants by the awarding of certificates or small mementos. It is important that the organisation acknowledges the commitment of the participants. Write an account of the launch for the company journal.

Establish organisational goals

Clearly state the program goals. These also need to be documented in the support material. The goals of the program will have influenced the selection, matching and expectations of the participants.

Typical goals of mentoring programs that I have been involved with include the following.

- To provide one-to-one support for newly appointed leaders
- To provide opportunities for aspiring leaders to develop skills in management and administration, collaborative decision making, and interpersonal relationships and communication
- To provide collegiate support for leaders in the first year of their appointment
- To provide support and advancement opportunities for women in the organisation
- To provide motivation and renewal opportunities for experienced leaders
- To provide learning opportunities for staff identified with the potential for accelerated advancement within the organisation

Non-negotiable roles and responsibilities

Each organisation will have determined some non-negotiable aspects of the program. These might include aspects such as the minimum number of meetings between pairs, attendance at training sessions and the completion of particular documentation. The length of the formal relationship will be outlined. Most programs will occur over a minimum period of six months. In this time it is usually expected that pairs would meet a minimum of six times.

The organisation will also determine accountability mechanisms for each participant.

An important but often overlooked member of the mentoring process is the mentee's line manager or boss. Each stakeholder in the process—the mentor, mentee and boss— needs to be very clear about the program expectations, roles and responsibilities of the players and what impact participating in this program will have on the mentee's current workload expectations.

Best practice for mentoring relationships

Effective mentoring relationships have some common elements. The mentors have expertise or knowledge in their field; the ability to exert some influence on behalf of the mentee; a genuine interest in the mentee's growth and development; a commitment to the relationship; the ability to share credit; and highly developed communication skills.

Make it clear to the mentors why they were initially chosen, how they are expected to behave and the functions that they are likely to perform. Mentors should be prepared to:
- assist in career planning;
- provide specific skills training;

- observe behaviour and provide feedback;
- act as a source of information on the organisation's mission and goals;
- introduce the mentee to corporate structures, expectations and taboos; and
- act as a confidant in times of personal and work-related crisis.

Similarly, the orientation program should also include explanations of why the mentees were chosen and how they are expected to perform.

Skill training for mentees and mentors

Remember that mentees and mentors will have a degree of interpersonal skills. There are many, many quality books and resources available on the interpersonal skills needed by participants in mentoring relationships. Look at the specific needs of the participants in your program and design activities that will enhance the required skills. It is not expected that the skills training program will do anything more than provide a refresher course in some of the following: listening; giving and receiving advice; giving feedback; questioning; and negotiation. Later, in Chapter Five there are sample activities to strengthen some of these skills—see Activities 6, 14, 15, 16, and 17.

Developing a rapport between partners

In some programs partners will have chosen their own partner and know them reasonably well; in other cases partners will not have even met. The orientation program needs to provide activities that help the partners to quickly get to know each other. At the conclusion of the orientation the partners should have a basic understanding of their partner's background, current work and personal situation, future goals and values. Trust building and personal awareness activities are included in Chapter Five—see Activities 1, 2, 3, 4, and 5.

Personal working styles

An important aspect of the orientation phase is the time spent understanding each other's personal style. There are a number of indicators available that identify personal working styles. Organisations can choose to use a commercially available tool or use training activities that help the participants understand their own styles of operating, reflect on the impact of their own style and how they react to other styles of operating. Some commercially available tools are listed in Chapter Six. See also Activity 7. This is only an initial starting point. Program designers should research current tools, identify tools that have been used previously by participants, and assess the appropriateness of each tool for their target group of participants.

The Myers-Briggs Type Indicator (MBTI) is probably the best known of the commercially available tools. It is a very useful tool, but like many of these indicators, it does need to be administered by a suitably qualified person. However, there are many people available with such qualifications, which makes this tool quite accessible.

Current performance/competency

Any plan for the mentee's growth and development needs to be based on an accurate assessment of the mentee's current strengths and weaknesses.

Many organisations have their own appraisal system, and this information can be used in the mentoring process. If your organisation does not have an appraisal system, there are commercially available appraisal programs. For industry-specific appraisal programs, contact your professional body or industry training board. Competencies have been developed for most industry groups. There are also assessment tools available for generic leadership competencies which do not need a qualified administrator. Information on these leadership indicators (MARC and Seven Dimensions Skills Indicators) is included in Chapter Six.

The orientation program should require that the participants either conduct a performance appraisal or reflect on the data provided by the mentee's current performance appraisal. See also Activities 8 and 9.

Expectations and protocols

Each program has its own non-negotiable aspects, such as the minimum number of times partners will meet, training obligations, specific tools to be used. These will have been outlined in the pre-advertising and reiterated at the beginning of the orientation phase. For each pair, however, there are a number of other protocols and expectations that will need to be discussed, agreed and documented. These include the following.

- Meetings, including frequency, location and duration
- Who initiates contact
- Responsibility for setting agendas
- Information required by the mentee
- Information required by the mentor
- Expectations of the mentee's boss
- Expectations of the mentee for the mentor
- Expectations of the mentor for the mentee
- Main mentoring functions to be performed
- Protocols for observing each other
- Protocols for giving feedback

Program organisers will determine which of these expectations and protocols need to be agreed by the individual pairs. Include these as part of the orientation program. A sample document has been included in Chapter Six. See also Activities 11 and 12.

Goal setting, action planning and tracking progress

Participants might not be ready to agree on goals and determine the action plan during the orientation phase but the program needs to include strategies for these processes. The goals will be based on the outcomes of the performance appraisal process, the competency assessment or the personal career goals of the mentee.

The goals need to be SMART (that is, Specific, Measurable, Action-oriented, Realistic and Time- and resource-constrained).

Specific: Make the goal detailed, particular and focused. For example, 'Improve time management' is too general. 'Reduce the time taken in producing the monthly written report' is specific. 'Completing project tasks on time, with no more than one task per month requiring overtime' is specific.

Measurable: You need to be able to measure the level of achievement. For example, 'To be able to produce the monthly written reports in no more than four hours'.

Action-oriented: Goal statements include a description of the activity that will be performed. They include verbs such as increase, produce, demonstrate, investigate.

Realistic: The goal set must be achievable within the time-frame allowed. It must be challenging enough to motivate you, practical enough to be of real benefit, and achievable. It is no use deciding to produce reports in no more than four hours if it is currently taking you four days. To make this a realistic goal you would need to set a goal that might be 'Within twelve months to be able to produce reports in no more than four hours' and then set short-term goals to measure progress along the way.

Time- and resource-constrained: Your goal needs to recognise the time needed to achieve it. You need to take into account all of the constraints that might have an effect on how quickly you can achieve your goal. These might include aspects such as access to particular technology, training programs, the costs involved, family and other work commitments.

Participants need to be skilled in developing SMART goals. Few people are. Most of us are good at writing New Year's Eve goals—'To be a better person', for example. In work terms, typical New Year goals might be to communicate better, be less stressed, produce more widgets. SMART goals make us decide exactly what we want to achieve, by when, and how we will know that we have been successful.

Once goals have been agreed the pair will need to spend time planning exactly how the mentee will achieve these goals. The mentee needs to analyse each goal and determine what new knowledge and skills are needed to achieve the goal and then develop an action plan to gain the knowledge and skills.

Action plans document your strategy for achieving your goal. Now that the goal is specific and measurable it should be easier to decide what needs to occur. The action plan should include tasks you need to do, information you need to gain, skills you need to gain and resources that will assist you. The action plan also includes your strategy for gaining the information and skills that you have identified. This could be through networking, reading, further courses, discussions or time with the mentor.

The action plan also needs to be very specific. For example, 'Improve computer skills' is too open ended a goal. The following are very different computer skills that are specific and targeted to improve the use of technology. 'Learn keyboarding skills so that I can touch type at a speed of 40 words per minute.' 'Learn PowerPoint™ so that I can design my own presentations that incorporate multimedia.' 'Improve my knowledge of Internet search engines so that I can locate appropriate sources of national and international data within 30 minutes.'

Once you have identified the skills or knowledge needed, the next step is to decide on the strategy for gaining that knowledge or skill. To learn PowerPoint™ you might decide to attend a training course, complete the self-paced training in the manual, purchase a self-paced computer program, or work with a coach from your workplace who you know is skilled in this area.

Allow time in the orientation program for goal setting and action planning (see Activities 18 and 19) and train participants in setting SMART goals.

If the goals are SMART goals it will be easy to track progress. Include both formal and informal strategies for keeping track of progress. Mentees need to be accountable to their mentor and the organisation. One of the ways that the organisation can keep track of each pair is through the program facilitator. Remember, the program facilitator will be making contact with each participant regularly during each phase of the program. Provide strategies for pairs to informally keep track of progress. These could include keeping a reflective journal, developing personal checklists, and periodic reviews of the action plan.

A reflective journal is a diary of events, incidents and your thoughts about them. They take many forms. Some people write in their journal at a regular time each day, say at the end of the working day. Others write following particular events, such as after each team meeting. To make reflective journals useful, there are a few points to keep in mind. Writing in the journal should not be a chore. Don't worry about spelling, punctuation, grammar—just write in whatever form you find easiest. This could be point form or jottings or complete sentences or paragraphs. The journal is for your use, not for anyone else.

If you are working on your communication skills, you might decide to keep a diary note of particular times when your communication style worked well, and times when things did not work out as well as you'd hoped. Use the journal to reflect on and analyse these incidents.

Reports from previous pairs and evaluation

At the conclusion of the orientation program include a report from a pair who have already participated in a mentoring program. Ask them to speak candidly for 10 to 15 minutes about their experiences and then take questions from the group. You need to choose the pair carefully. They need to be prepared to talk openly about the strengths of the program and any pitfalls that they experienced. You might consider inviting two pairs to provide balance. If at all possible, invite a pair rather than an individual mentor and a mentee from a different pair. Brief the pair by asking them to speak on the benefits of the mentoring relationship and any pitfalls that they experienced, and to describe any events which significantly altered the relationship. It is also useful to ask the mentor and the mentee if they have any advice which they would give to a new mentor/mentee.

Ask each participant to complete an evaluation proforma of the program to date. This should cover initial advertising, selection procedures, matching procedures, and the training program. At this stage it is important that these evaluations are seen as initial indicators of strengths and weaknesses in the program design and orientation. Accurate judgements on each aspect cannot be made at this early stage of the program. Perceptions will change.

A sample evaluation proforma is given in Chapter Six.

Once the evaluations are collated, initial recommendations for following programs and/or modifications to this program can be made. These will be confirmed or varied after the completion of the program, with later evaluations also being taken into consideration.

Mid-cycle

Three to four months after the orientation program, participants appreciate spending time together as a group. Depending on the length of the formal mentoring relationship, there might be more than one mid-cycle meeting of participants. The purpose of this time together is to share strategies that have been working for them as mentors or mentees, discuss with other mentors or mentees problems that they are facing, renegotiate learning goals, and participate in more training activities aimed at further developing the relationship. Training ideas have been included in Chapter Five. See Activities 20, 21, 22, 23, 24 and 25.

As with the orientation program, the mid-cycle support program should be formally evaluated. A sample evaluation proforma appears in Chapter Six. Again, once the evalusations have been collated, recommendations for improvement can be made.

Relationship closure

From the organisation's point of view, formal mentoring programs should have a finite length. Some pairs will choose to continue the relationship beyond the formal program. In fact, this is probably the overall aim of the program, but it is important that when participants volunteer their commitment is for a specific period of time. If there is no formal conclusion to the relationship it could fade away without a sense of closure. A formal session that concludes the program allows participants to express their appreciation to their partner, acknowledges the contribution that the mentors have made to the organisation, and marks the end of the formal relationship and commitment.

Bring all of the partners together for a final meeting. Provide an opportunity for the pairs to share significant moments and experiences with each other. Organise some method of recording these stories as part of the evaluation. There should also be an opportunity for both mentors and mentees to reflect on their own career development and set some new-long term goals. You probably won't allocate time to complete this task in the final session but refer to this as a 'Where to from here?' strategy.

This final session is an opportunity for the organisation to reward both partners, but particularly the mentors who may have less tangible gains from participating in this program. The reward can come in many forms. It might be a certificate, commemorative plaque, or an write-up in the company newsletter. The reward does not have to be anything, it might just be a thank you from significant leaders within the company and formal recognition of the contribution of the participants. See Activities 26, 27, 28 and 29.

Most organisations will choose to conduct the final evaluation of the impact of the program at the formal conclusion to the program. It is useful to ask participants to re-evaluate the initial advertising, selection and matching procedures and the training activities from the orientation phase, and the training program support from the program facilitator and impact of the program from the mid-cycle phase, as well as evaluating the relationship closure phase. (Sample evaluation proformas appear in Chapter Six.) Participants' perceptions may change during the course of the program, and a much more reliable assessment of the various processes, procedures and training activities is usually given at the end of the program.

Follow-up evaluation

To obtain accurate data about the success and influence of the program you need to continue the evaluation process for at least one year beyond the formal conclusion of the program. However, few organisations are prepared to resource the evaluation process to that extent.

The final evaluation from the formal conclusion to the relationship will provide data on the strengths and weaknesses of the program to date. What will be missing though is the impact that the program actually had at least twelve months following the program conclusion. In my experience this is some of the most valuable data. Some relationships that ended on a high had an initial but not long-term impact. Other relationships were 'quiet achievers'. Most relationships will not have an immediate impact, as mentoring is a long-term process. The formal program aims to introduce the concept and skills—the real mentoring is likely to take place long after the initial structured relationship phase. If the organisation does not track pairs beyond the program this information will be lost. A sample follow-up evaluation proforma appears in Chapter Six.

Final recommendations

Recommendations can be made from the evaluation data to date. This will now include:
- Orientation phase data
    - initial advertising
    - selection procedures
    - matching procedures
    - orientation training program
    - recommendations
- Mid-cycle phase data
    - mid-cycle training program
    - support from the program facilitator
    - recommendations
    - impact of the program
- Relationship closure data
    - initial advertising
    - selection procedures
    - matching procedures
    - training program
    - support from program facilitator
    - impact of the program
    - final session
- Final evaluation data
    - impact of the program

Cross reference the evaluations that were made at the earlier stages with the re-evaluations. Most organisations will make their final recommendations at this stage. The true value of the program is more accurately assessed after a follow-up evaluation.

CHAPTER FIVE

Activities

Orientation ● Mid-Cycle ● Relationship Closure

Orientation

Activities 1–18 are appropriate for use in the orientation training program or by individual pairs during the early stages of their relationship.

Activity **Uncommon commonalities**

Purpose

To stimulate a discussion between partners that will require them to share unusual and personal data about themselves.

Approximate time

10 minutes

Resources needed

Nil

Steps

Participants are asked to share personal information about themselves with their partner until they believe that they have found something that they have in common that no other pair in the room will have in common. For example, members of one pair discovered that they each had a brother who died of illness as a teenager. Another couple discovered that they had both been hot-air ballooning across the Serengeti.

Developing trust

Your partner has the right to pass on any question. If you choose to answer a question, do so honestly.

1. **Describe your different responsibilities.**

2. **What gives you the greatest sense of job satisfaction?**

3. **What do you regard as your major strengths?**

4. **What areas would you like to focus on for improvement?**

5. **Describe the area of responsibility that you find most frustrating.**

6. **What helps you most in your work?**

7. **What hinders you from achieving your goals?**

8. **Are you happy in your present job? Why? Why not?**

Activity	**2**	**Developing trust**

Purpose

To initiate a discussion between the partners that requires a level of self-disclosure and develops trust.

Approximate time

20–30 minutes

Resources needed

Worksheet for each participant

Steps

Mentors and mentees take turns in asking and answering the questions on the worksheet. They may be asked in any order.

Activity	**3**	**Passion Chart**

Purpose

To stimulate personal reflection and/or discussion on aspects of our work life that provide job satisfaction, frustration and stress.

This activity can be used by individual program participants as a self-reflective tool or by mentoring pairs early in the relationship. It can also be used during the orientation program to develop a rapport between the pairs.

Approximate time

30–60 minutes

Resources needed

Worksheets for each participant

Steps

Participants categorise different aspects of their job, using the worksheets, and then develop an action plan (see Activity 18).

Passion Chart

Reflect on your current work. Using the Passion Chart categorise your work in four ways:

1 **Things that you like and do well**

2 **Things that you like but do not do well**

3 **Things that you do well but do not like**

4 **Things that you do not like and do not do well**

Spend some time privately reflecting on the following questions or discuss them with your partner.

How many work tasks fell into each category?

Which tasks take up the most time?

Our main source of job satisfaction comes from work that we like and do well. We frequently find that we spend less and less time in this quadrant. It is quite common for people to find that they have been promoted away from doing any of this work.

Aspects of our work that we like but do not do particularly well should form the basis of our professional development plan. These can easily be moved into the like and do well category.

All jobs have aspects that we do not like. In many cases we have developed skills in these areas even though we do not particularly like that aspect of our work. Unfortunately as we move up the organisational ladder we often find that we do more of this work and less of the work that we like and do well. This is a trap. This category of work provides an ideal opportunity to delegate or train someone else. The ideal is to find a team member who likes these tasks but is not particularly good at them.

The final category is don't like and don't do well. People who have many aspects of their work that fall into this category quickly become disillusioned, burnt out or stressed. We can all accept some aspects in this quadrant, but it cannot be the dominant quadrant. We need to look at the tasks that fall into this quadrant and put them into two categories: things I just need to accept as part of this job; and things that can change. Now look at the things that can change. Some of these you alone can change and others involve others.

Develop an action plan to change the things for which you are solely responsible. Develop a second action plan for those that involve others.

When I reflect on my own Passion Chart the placement of my computer skills has moved quite significantly. In 1985 computers were coming into the workplace. I didn't like them and I certainly did not manage them well. It wasn't long before I had to spend significant amounts of time on the computer. I attended courses and gained some skills. It wasn't long before I found that I actually enjoyed using the computer. I still was not good at it but eventually even that changed. While the computer remains a tool to do the real work that I like and am good at, I now actually like using the computer and am reasonably proficient with it for the things I need it for.

	Like	**Don't Like**
Do Well	1	2
Don't Do Well	3	4

Activity **4** Snakes and ladders

Purpose

To explore what is important to each of us and why.
To provide a basis for discussions on making time for each aspect of our lives.

Approximate time

20–30 minutes

Resources needed

Worksheet for each participant

Steps

Each participant fills in the worksheet, then uses the worksheet as a basis for discussion.

Think about the aspects of your life listed below. Delete children and/or partner if these are not appropriate to you. Draw a ladder with the appropriate number of rungs. Starting with the top rung, write down each of these components of your life in their order of importance, with the most important on the top rung.

Discuss your rankings with your partner.

Discuss how much time you gave to each of these aspects in the last week/month.

Children

Friends

Partner

Extended family

Me

Work

Belief

Activity 5 — Opening up the window

Purpose

To develop trust between partners by stimulating dialogue that requires a degree of self-disclosure.

Approximate time

At least one hour

Resources needed

Question booklets for each participant

Booklets will need to be prepared for the activity.

Each section of instructions should appear on a separate page. Each open-ended statement should appear on a separate page. If you make each booklet page 10 cm × 21 cm you will fit 3 pages on an A4-size piece of paper. The instructions appear in italics, and the questions in normal print. There should be 21 pages altogether, counting a title page with the Activity name.

A room that is large enough to allow the participants to sit facing each other with nothing between them. They should not be able to hear the conversations of others.

Steps

Discuss the ground rules which are also printed in the front of each booklet.

Pairs follow the instructions in the booklets. The time needed will vary, but allow at least one hour. Some pairs might wish to continue the discussions much longer. Allow participants to take the booklets away and complete them in their own time.

Worksheet **5**	**Opening up the window**

This exercise is designed to facilitate getting to know another person on a fairly intimate level. The discussion items are open-ended statements and can be completed at whatever level of self-disclosure one wishes. The following ground rules should govern this exercise.

- All of the data discussed should be kept strictly confidential.
- You may decline to complete any statement.
- You can stop at any time that you, or your partner become uncomfortable.
- Don't look ahead in the booklet.

Page 2
- Both partners respond to each of the following four open-ended statements before moving on to the next one.
- The statements are to be completed in the order in which they appear.

Page 3
My full name is

Page 4
My qualifications are

Page 5
The reason why I am here is

Page 6
Right now I am feeling

Page 7
These instructions refer to all the remaining open-ended statements.

One of the most important skills in getting to know another person is listening. In order to check on your ability to understand what your partner is communicating, the two of you should go through the procedure one at a time.

Decide which of you is to speak first.

The first speaker is to complete each of the following statements, adding another sentence or two.

The listener reflects back the speaker's comments after each third question. Try to reflect back the general content, specific facts and the feelings reflected in the statements.

Swap roles and the listener then becomes the speaker.

Page 8
When I am feeling anxious in a new situation I usually

Page 9
I am happiest when

Page 10
Right now I am feeling

Page 11
I like to be just a follower when

Page 12
When I am alone I usually

Page 13
In crowds I

Page 14
In a group I usually get most involved when

Page 15
I am rebellious when

Page 16
The emotion I find most difficult to control is

Page 17
My most frequent daydreams are about

Page 18
I believe in

Page 19
I regret

Page 20
I am most proud of

Page 21
When I think about the future I see myself

Activity **6** **Receiving feedback**

Purpose

To establish an understanding of how each member of a pair would prefer to give and receive feedback.

Approximate time

20 minutes

Resources needed

Worksheet for each participant

Steps

Each participant reads the worksheet and ticks the five statements that best describe how they prefer to receive feedback. Each participant then ranks those five statements from one to five, with one being the most important. It is important that the facilitator stresses that it is how they prefer to receive feedback not give feedback.

The mentoring pairs compare their rankings.

Discuss the comparisons as a whole group. It is common to find that some pairs will have similar rankings and others quite different. Participants are also likely to either place 'Given with care' or 'Directly or Fully expressed' high in their ranking. There is no right or wrong answer.

Discuss the different ways in which we often prefer to give and receive feedback. When we give feedback we often like to give it with care, sometimes with so much care that the receiver does not receive a clear message. Ask the question 'Whose need is being met when we give feedback?' The answer must be the need of the person receiving the feedback. It is important that both mentors and mentees understand their partner's preferred way of giving and receiving feedback.

Worksheet **6**	**Receiving Feedback**

Given with care	To be useful, feedback requires the giver to feel concern and care for the person receiving the feedback—to want to help, not to hurt the other person.
Invited by the recipient	Feedback is most effective when the receiver has invited the comments. This provides a platform for openness and some guidelines; it also gives the receiver an opportunity to identify and explore particular areas of concern.
Freedom of choice to change	Feedback is most readily accepted when the receiver is supported to change but does not feel compelled to change.
Directly expressed	Good feedback is specific and deals clearly with particular incidents and behaviour. It is direct, open and concrete.
Fully expressed	Effective feedback requires more than a bald statement of facts. Feelings also need to be expressed so that the receiver can judge the full impact of their behaviour.
Non-evaluative	Specific behaviour is commented on rather than personal value judgements about that behaviour.
Well-timed	The most useful feedback is given when the receiver is receptive to it and is sufficiently close to the particular event being discussed for it to be fresh in their mind.
Readily actionable	Effective feedback centres around behaviour that can be changed. Feedback concerning matters outside the control of the receiver is useless.
Checked and clarified	If possible, feedback should be clarified to explore differences in perceptions.

Activity 7 — Styles and preferences

Purpose

To explore how we prefer to solve problems, learn or look for challenges. This activity can be used by program facilitators with all participants or by individual mentoring pairs. This does not require a qualified administrator.

Approximate time

10 minutes

Resources needed

Worksheet for each participant

Steps

Participants use the worksheet to determine their preferred style, then discuss their preferences with their partner.

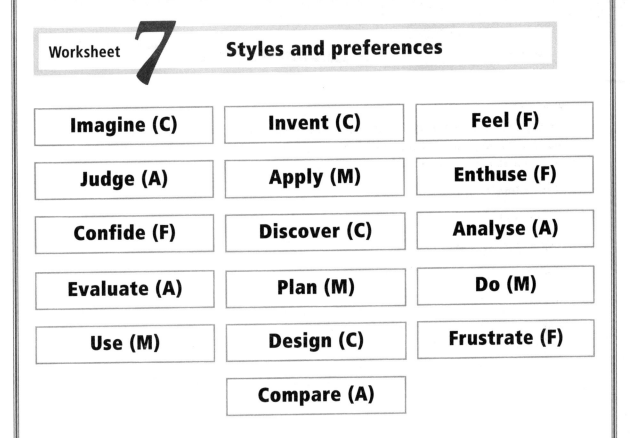

Imagine (C)   Invent (C)   Feel (F)

Judge (A)   Apply (M)   Enthuse (F)

Confide (F)   Discover (C)   Analyse (A)

Evaluate (A)   Plan (M)   Do (M)

Use (M)   Design (C)   Frustrate (F)

Compare (A)

Circle the four words that appeal to you the most in describing your approach to life.

Discuss the words that you chose with your partner.

You will notice that each of the words has a letter beside it. These letters relate to preferences in style. A stands for Analyse; C for Create; M for Make; and F for Feel.

Determine the preference style for each of your chosen words. We all have preferences in both learning and problem solving. We also need to be able to use skills from the non-preferred styles. Analytical people usually like to be logical, sequential, looking at all sides of the problem or issue. Creative preferences indicate that you have unusual approaches to issues, seeing a different angle. People with a practical bent (those who choose 'Make') value ideas and activities that are immediately useful. They are task committed and like to get on with it. People with high emotional preferences (those who choose 'Feel') have a deep understanding of themselves and others.

We all need to be able to use each of the four styles, but we usually find that we operate best in one or two styles. That's why they are called preferences.

My preferred style is creative, with analytical close behind. I have worked to develop the practical and my least preferred style, emotional. Discuss your preferences with your partner and how you have developed/will develop the remaining areas.

Activity **8** Self-appraisal

Purpose

To provide a guide for self reflection by the mentee or to stimulate discussion between pairs around the performance of the mentee.

Approximate time

20–30 minutes

Resources needed

Worksheet for each participant

Steps

Use the questions on the worksheet as discussion starters.

Activity **9** Reviewing performance

Purpose

To stimulate discussion about the mentee's performance. One worksheet can be used to reflect on past performance, the other to plan improvements for the future. This activity can be used as part of the training program or given to pairs to complete in their own time.

Approximate time

At least 1 hour

Resources needed

Worksheet for each participant

Steps

Pairs use the questions on the worksheet to stimulate discussion around the mentee's past or future performance. The mentor should use these questions as a starting point only. Adapt the questions to suit the needs of the mentee and your style. If these questions seem too formal, change them. Listen to the mentee's responses and follow-up with an appropriate question, not necessarily the next. This will show that you really are listening.
or
Mentees use these questions as a tool to stimulate self reflection on job performance and directions. Discuss these reflections with your mentor.

Worksheet	**Self appraisal**

I see my job-related strengths as

I think that   has been working well.

I could build on this by

My most significant achievement in the last twelve months is

The aspect of my work that is of greatest concern to me is

I've tried to address this by

My key work goal for the next twelve months is to

The aspect of my work that most frustrates me is

This could be improved by

The thing that would make the greatest difference to my work would be

I would like support to

I would be able to support others to

I would like to gain the following skills

I would like to have the following experiences

I would like to increase my knowledge of

9a Reviewing past performance

The following are some questions to help in the mentee's self assessment. They will assist in the identification of areas for self improvement.

Introductory
- What are your immediate thoughts about your job?
- How do you feel about the past year/other appropriate period?

Job
- What do you see as the main purpose/responsibilities of your job?
- What do you see as the highest priority for you in your job?
- How has the job changed/developed over the past year/period?
- Which aspects of your job do you most/least like, find least/most interesting?
- Which areas of your work do you think have gone well/do you feel pleased about?
- What do you think has brought about your achievements/caused your problems?

Relationships
- Who are your main work contacts?
- Who directly affects the way you perform?
- Who are most directly affected by the way you perform?
- What support and assistance do you receive from/give to others?
- How do you feel about your working relationships with colleagues/manager/others/me?

Personal
- How do you rate yourself in terms of job skills/problem solving/communication skills/leadership?
- What skills do you have that are not being fully used in your job?
- How do you feel you have changed/progressed/developed/improved over the past year/period?
- How do you feel about problem areas?
- What would you say you have learnt from the last year's experiences?
- What, with hindsight, would you do differently?

Concluding
- What else would you like to raise?
- What do you consider to be the most important/significant areas for development/improvement in the coming year/period?

9b # Improving future performance

Introductory

- How do you anticipate your job could/should develop or change in emphasis over the next year/other appropriate period?
- How would you like to see your working relationships develop/change?
- What do you think can be done to improve things/make things even better?
- What do you feel should be given priority attention?

Job/relationships

Use the following questions to reflect on both your job and your work relationships.

- What could you do to help things along?
- How will you go about it?
- What help do you need from others/me?
- What additional knowledge/skills would you find useful?
- What training/development/projects would help?
- What do you see as appropriate targets/objectives for the coming year/period?
- How will you measure success/progress?
- What could get in the way of success?
- What could be done to overcome such obstacles?
- What alternatives are open to you?

Personal

- How do you see your future with this organisation?
- What particular career aspirations do you have?
- What do you see as the next step/s in your personal development?

Concluding

- What other issues would you like to raise?
- How do you feel about what we have discussed?
- What do you see as the main targets/objectives/action plans we need to agree?
- When should we meet again to do this?

Activity **10** What makes an effective mentor?

Purpose

To stimulate discussion on the qualities and characteristics of effective mentors.

Approximate time

20 minutes

Resources needed

Worksheet for each participant

Steps

All participants read the list on the worksheet and rank the qualities and characteristics that they see as most important for mentors to have, in order from one (as most important) to ten. Mentors and mentees form separate groups to discuss their individual rankings and develop a ranked group list.

All participants reform into one large group and discuss the similarities and differences between the two groups' rankings.

What makes an effective mentor?

People are often reluctant to volunteer to be mentors because they feel that mentors are 'super beings'. This is not the case. It is possible to identify the qualities and characteristics that are important for successful mentoring relationships. Some of these are:

role model	**willingness to be a mentor**
guide	**experienced**
supporter	**knowledgeable**
advisor	**interested**
trusted counsellor	**accessible**
leader	**shares resources**
friend	**observes confidentiality**
listener	**shows mutual respect**
networker	**shows affection**

Rank this list from one to ten. Add any qualities or characteristics which are missing.

Activity **11**

Events and people that impacted on my leadership style

Purpose

To prompt mentors to reflect on people and events that have had an impact on them. To help mentors to understand their potential impact on their mentee.

Approximate time

20 minutes

Resources needed

Whiteboard and markers
Butcher paper

Steps

Mentors work in groups of three. One member of the group acts as a scribe, recording the group's comments on each category on a separate piece of butcher paper.

Each group discusses people and events that have had an impact on them at three different stages in their career:

- as a new *engineer* (replace with appropriate job type)
- in early leadership roles
- as a senior manager

Discuss the three lists from each group and note any similarities or patterns on the whiteboard.

Groups will usually identify that it is people who had the significant impact, rather than events. Discuss what it was about those people that was different or significant. You will usually find that it was that the significant person believed in them and encouraged them to take risks and push themselves. They provided motivation, support and counselling.

What are the messages here for mentors? What were the most influential and supportive behaviours? What were the significant times for providing different types of support?

What are the messages for mentees? Have there been times when mentors did not make full use of support that was available? Why? How can mentors increase the likelihood of useful support being provided?

Activity 12 — I think I know, what you think I think

Purpose

To raise for open discussion the perceptions and expectations of mentors and mentees.

Approximate time

At least 30 minutes

Resources needed

Butcher paper and markers

Steps

Form two groups, one of mentors and one of mentees.
Each group is to appoint a scribe and record their brainstorm responses to the following two questions.

> What do you think the mentees want from the mentors?
> What do you think the mentors want from the mentees?

Following the brainstorm, the groups join together to discuss the following.

> What each group expects from their partner;
> What each group thought that their partner would expect.

Compare the actual expectations and the perceived expectations.

Patterns for noting and commenting:

> Was there a match between the actual expectations and the perceived expectations?
> What were the differences between the expectations of the mentors and mentees?
> What patterns emerge from the lists of expectations?

Workshop materials

Questions prepared on butcher paper.

Activity **13** Coaching to build skills

Purpose

To avoid common traps of coaching situations.

Approximate time

15 minutes

Resources needed

Whiteboard and markers

Steps

List on a whiteboard common problems managers face when trying to coach new skills. These are likely to include the following:
- Employee's base-level skills are different to what was expected. They either already have the skills or their skill level is several levels lower than expected.
- The employee becomes confused.
- The employee does not use the skills following the training.

Discuss the basic coaching cycle of
1. Explain—The person needs to know what the skill is, why it is important and how it fits into the rest of the work being done.
2. Demonstrate—The demonstration should be in an authentic work situation. When this is not appropriate or possible the task should be modelled in a simulated situation as close to the real work conditions as possible.
3. Practise—Ensure that the person practises the task. When they are practising, encourage them. Be tolerant. Not everyone learns at the same rate or in the same way.
4. Feedback—Give feedback that is clear and specific. If necessary give more than one practice opportunity.

Managers as coaches fall into common traps:

Common mistake	What to do
Not checking the person's skill level	Check and build on existing knowledge
Confusing the person being coached	Explain the task in small logical steps
Not responding to possible confusion	Read non-verbal language and regularly check for understanding
Explaining the skill in isolation	Place the skill in the learner's context

Activity **14** **Listening goals**

Purpose

To encourage the mentor to actively listen by asking questions.

Approximate time

10 minutes

Resources needed

Nil

Steps

The mentor can introduce this activity at any stage in the relationship. Every time the mentor asks a question during a discussion they gain a point. Every time they make a statement about themselves they lose a point. The mentor's aim is to gain as many points as possible in ten minutes.

The mentor might discuss this activity with their mentee and ask them to record the number of questions and the number of statements made by the mentor at random times in the relationship. The mentee is unlikely to initiate the process.

Activity **15** **General, specific, feelings**

Purpose

To practise the skill of focused listening.

Approximate time

20 minutes

Resources needed

Nil

Steps

Pairs sit facing each other. Ask the mentees to describe to their mentor their most significant achievement to date, their most embarrassing moment, or their most vivid childhood memory.

The mentor listens for general information, specific details and feelings. Mentors then feedback their understanding of the incident discussing the general, specific and feelings.

Activity 16 — Questions, questions and more questions

Purpose

To broaden the range of question types used by mentors.

Approximate time

15 minutes

Resources needed

Whiteboard and markers
Worksheet for each pair

Steps

Separate the mentors and mentees. While the mentees are working on a separate activity, discuss the types of questions that we commonly use with the mentors. Most people rely on asking closed questions, which can be answered with a yes or no. We need to broaden our repertoire of questions to include probing, reminder, linking, leading, limited choice, open and closed questions. Discuss each type of question and identify situations where each would be most appropriate.

List each question type on one side of the whiteboard. Beside each question type list times in the mentoring relationship that each question type would be most appropriate. Brief the mentors for the activity. The mentees will not know what the mentor is trying to achieve.

Mentees join the group and sit with their mentor. They are told that their partner will be discussing some issues with them to help get to know them a bit better. They do not have to answer any question but what they do choose to answer should be answered honestly. Mentors will ask their partner questions to ascertain the situation or person who has had the greatest impact on their partner's learning. This could be someone in their early childhood, school or career. At the conclusion of the discussion/questioning the mentor should be able to describe the person or incident, the impact that they/it had and the significance of the impact.

Following the discussions, pairs use the workshop sheet of question types to discuss what questions were asked, how useful each question type was, what question types were not used and why.

Questions, questions and more questions

Probing Questions

Go on ...

Tell me more about ...

Give me a typical example...

What precisely happened?

What specifically did you do/say?

What was the outcome?

What else could have been done?

How did it arise?

How did you handle it?

How was it resolved?

How often/regularly did this happen?

How important/significant do you feel
 it is?

How strongly do you feel about it?

How could it have been handled better?

How do you mean?

When/where did this take place?

Who was involved?

Who else was affected/feels the same?

Why do you think this is/feel this
 way/say that?

Limited choice questions

Are you going to do ... or ...?

Will you speak to... or will I?

Reminder questions

You mentioned previously that ...

Could you remind me again of what
 happened when ...

Linking questions

You mentioned that ...?

How do you see us being able to
 improve...?

Leading questions

Don't you think that ...?

Shouldn't you have ...?

Open questions

How are you feeling?

What might happen if ...?

Closed questions

Have ...?

Do ...?

Can ...?

Did ...?

Would you agree that ...?

Activity 17 — Listening skills test

Purpose

To provide a checklist for participants to evaluate their own listening skills.

Approximate time

10 minutes

Resources needed

Worksheet for each participant

Steps

Participants complete the worksheet and discuss responses with their partner or with the group. In many cases participants will answer 'It depends. I can't say a categorical yes or no.' Draw out from them the things that influence how they respond when listening.

Activity 18 — Action plan

Purpose

To assist pairs in the process of developing an action plan.

Approximate time

60–90 minutes

Resources needed

At least 1 worksheet per pair

Steps

As program facilitator, complete a sample action planning proforma like the one following. Work through each step of the process with the group, providing suitable examples appropriate to your group.

Each mentee completes one action plan per goal, with the assistance of their mentor. At least one action plan should be completed in the training program to ensure that the pairs understand the process.

Worksheet 17 — Listening skills test

Question	Yes	No
When you arrive at a conference or training workshop do you aim to sit at the front?		
At meetings, do you take notes and refer to them later?		
When you are listening to someone do you ask questions?		
Do you find that your mind wanders when you are listening to particular people?		
Have you ever had someone say to you, 'You're not listening'?		
When you are listening to someone do you move so that you can see their facial expression?		
If someone is saying something you disagree with do you always let them finish before giving your opinion?		
Can you remember all of the conversations that you had yesterday?		
Do you listen more attentively to people who you find attractive or those in a senior position to you?		
Can you empathise with other people's points of view even when they are radically different to yours?		
Do you encourage people when they are speaking to you by using appropriate body language?		
Do you check your understanding of what is being said during the conversation?		
Can you list barriers to listening?		

| Activity **18** cont'd | **Action plan** |

Sample Action Plan

Area of focus
For example, communication, interpersonal skills, managing resources, supervising

SMART goal
Clearly worded goal that is specific, measurable, achievable, realistic and time-constrained.

Knowledge to be developed	
What?	How?
What specific knowledge do you need to achieve this goal?	How will you gain this knowledge, for example, reading, seminars, observation

Skills to be gained	
What?	How?
What specific skills do you need to achieve this goal?	How will you gain these skills, for example, discussions, coaching

Action plan for the goal

What are you going to do? This will include how you intend to gain new knowledge and skills and other tasks that need to be completed in order to achieve this goal.
For example,
Join the Australian Institute of Management.
Attend meetings at least 3 times each year.
Read AIM journal.
Read at least 1 management article each month. Summarise and discuss with a colleague.
Conduct reflection on where we have come from and where we are heading to present to the November board meeting.
Observe Fred briefing staff on current directions in business. Seek coaching tips.
Prepare draft speaking notes and discuss with Fred.
Trial briefing with board.

Area of focus

SMART goal

Knowledge to be developed
What?

How?

Skills to be gained
What?

How?

Action plan for the goal

Mid-cycle

Activities 19–25 are appropriate to use during the mid-cycle training program or by individual pairs as their relationship develops.

| Activity | **19** | **Personal professional development planning** |

Purpose

To stimulate reflection on the mentee's career plans and act as a focus for discussions on these plans with their mentor.

Approximate time

At least 30 minutes

Resources needed

Worksheet for each participant
Reflective journal

Steps

Mentees use the questions on the worksheet to reflect on their career goals. Mentees record their reflections in their journal for discussions with their mentor.

What is my long-term goal?

What are my strengths?

What skills do I need?

What experiences should I have?

What are my short-term goals?

What is my professional development strategy?

Activity 20 — Real plays—getting it right next time

Purpose

To practise interpersonal skills required by the mentee for a specific purpose.

Approximate time

45–60 minutes

Resources needed

Nil

Steps

Role plays should be initiated by the mentor at appropriate times in the relationship. Mentees are likely to avoid role plays as few people enjoy them. In many situations it will be the best method of quickly gaining the skills needed to handle a specific, real incident.

When role plays are on the agenda the mentor should use the following guidelines.

- Hypothetical role plays are of very limited value. The true value of role plays lies in basing them around real scenarios. The time to use a 'real' play is when the mentee has a curly issue to handle, such as telling an employee that they are about to be out-placed, or resolving a conflict situation between team members. Ask the mentee to describe the situation and focus on the specific skills needed to handle the issue. Conflict resolution is not specific. Identify strategies for handling the situation. Describe other factors impacting on the situation, such as one of the people involved has been highly emotional since his wife was diagnosed with a terminal illness, the other person involved is a new staff member employed after a long period of unemployment.
- Agree on strategies for handling the situation. Discuss specific feedback to be given and the most important verbal and non-verbal messages to be given.
- Allow sufficient time to get into the real play. During the initial practice allow either party to stop the action and replay events at any stage. The whole idea of the role play is to get it right when it is the real play. This is the time to say 'I'm not happy with the way this is going. Let's do it again.'
- Keep practising until the mentee feels confident.
- Following the actual incident, ask the mentee to spend time reflecting on how they handled the situation. Then the pair discuss:
    What worked well?
    What would you do differently?
    What do you need to do now?

Activity 21 — Reviewing our relationship

Purpose

To stimulate reflective discussion on the relationship to date and future directions.

Approximate time

Up to 30 minutes

Resources needed

Reflective journals

Steps

Ask each participant to consider the following. Use the reflective journal to record initial thoughts.

- In your role as a mentor or mentee identify any significant moment/s during the past three months.
- Describe what happened, why it was significant and what impact it had on you.
- Discuss these reflections with your partner.
- Where do you plan to go from here in your mentor relationship?
- Where do you plan to go from here with your goals?

Discuss these reflections with your partner.

Activity 22 Sharing secrets

Purpose

To provide a framework for feedback discussions to increase the mentor's and mentee's knowledge of themselves and their partner.

Approximate time

At least 30 minutes

Resources needed

Whiteboard and markers

Steps

Draw the quadrant diagram.

Explain the four quadrants.

1. Things about me and my behaviour known both to me and to others.
2. Things about me that others know but are unknown to me.
3. Things about me that I know but are unknown to others.
4. Things about me that are unknown both to me and to others.

	What I know about myself	What I don't know about myself
What you know about me	1	2
What you don't know about me	3	4

As we spend time with someone we reveal information about ourselves, find out information about ourselves, find out information about our partner and reveal information to them about themselves. Our understanding of ourselves and others is greatly enhanced the more we are prepared to share about ourselves and the more we are prepared to take on board from others.

Partners sit facing each other, and take turns in sharing information with each other.

Each person must share with their partner two pieces of information. Participants share information which they are now comfortable for their partner to know. The confidentiality of information shared is to be respected.

1. Something I know about me that you don't know.
    Participants choose what to reveal—it might be their middle name, their secret wish, their greatest fear. It must be something that their partner does not already know about them.
2. Something I know about you that you don't know.
    Participants tell their partner something about themselves of which they are unaware. This should be positive and helpful. It might be something that was noticed during a visit to their workplace, the way they reacted in a particular situation.

Activity 23 Self-talk attitudes

Purpose

To stimulate discussion on helpful and unhelpful attitudes.

Approximate time

15 minutes

Resources needed

Worksheet for each pair

Steps

Pairs use the statements on the worksheets to stimulate discussion on negative self-talk.

Our attitudes contribute to negative self-talk. Use the following statements to reflect on your reactions.

Discuss these with your partner.

If I receive any criticism at all I see myself as a failure.

I attribute success to something other than my own abilities or talent.

A colleague of mine has been acting a bit funny lately and I assume that it was something I said or did.

The last project that I led did not go as well as I would have liked, so I am worried that my next project will also be a failure.

I label myself instead of describing a mistake that I have made ... for example, 'I'm such an idiot!' 'How could I have been such a fool?' 'Only an idiot would have ...'

My manager criticises my work. I find myself feeling angry and defensive.

Write down one or two negative self-talk statements you make to yourself when under pressure or when you have just been criticised.

Analyse the statements that you wrote down and rewrite them positively and pro-actively. For example,

My manager criticises my work. I will ask them to explain exactly what outcomes they expected and did not get. I will seek agreement on a course of action I need to take to:
a. remedy the current situation;
b. ensure that it will not occur again.

Activity 24 — Now and then

Purpose

To reflect on the past and present and where participants would like to be in five years' time.

Approximate time

At least 30 minutes

Resources needed

Worksheet for each participant

Steps

This activity can be conducted as a self-reflective activity by mentors or mentees, by mentoring pairs during the course of their relationship, or can be used as part of the training program.

Activity 25 — Personal task audit

Purpose

To provide a framework with which mentees can compare job or personal goals and the time allocated to achieving these in any given week. This activity can be completed during the mid-cycle training program or by mentees at any stage during the relationship.

Approximate time

At least 1 hour

Resources needed

Worksheet for each participant

Steps

Mentees use the worksheet to complete a personal task audit and, with their mentor's help, plan to use their time more effectively to achieve their goals.

Draw three pictures of yourself at different stages in your life. You might like to use images or things that represent you.

1.   You now.
2.   You in the past. Choose a time before you were working in this job. It might be you as a child, a new graduate, working in your first job.
3.   You in five years' time.

(You might choose to share these images with your mentoring partner.)

During the professional journey that each of us have made there have been many influences that have helped us. Take five minutes to reflect on the people and events that have helped shape you.

(You might choose to share these reflections with your mentoring partner.)

What knowledge, skills and experiences helped you to achieve your current position?

Revisit the last of the three images of yourself. Where do you want to be in five years? Write this as a career goal.

What knowledge, skills and experiences will you need to achieve this goal?

(You might choose to share these reflections with your mentoring partner.)

List your achievement goals in the appropriate boxes down the side of the worksheet.

List the tasks you completed in the previous week in the appropriate boxes along the top of the worksheet.

Reflect on each task as it relates to each goal or priority.

Using the coding printed on the worksheet, rank each task as having:

- a very strong positive influence, i.e., this task will bring me much closer to achieving this goal;
- a positive influence, i.e., this task brings me a little way towards achieving this goal;
- no influence, i.e., this task has nothing to do with my goals;
- a negative influence, i.e., this task actually blocks me achieving this goal;
- a missed opportunity, i.e., if I had approached this task in a different way it could have helped me to achieve this goal.

Discuss your reflections with your mentor. Are the work tasks that take up your time helping you to achieve your goals, having no impact on your goals or actually blocking the achievement of your goals?

What opportunities have been missed?

How can you achieve the most from your daily work program?

Tasks														
Goals														

● **++ve influence** ○ **+ve influence** ▲ **no influence** ✖ **–ve influence** ✔ **missed opportunity**

Relationship closure

It is important that the relationships come to a formal conclusion. This does not need to be a major event but some formal recognition and mark of appreciation need to be made. The organisation should recognise the contribution of all of the participants with a certificate or commemorative item. Some organisations ask mentees to nominate particular mentors for awards for contributions above and beyond the call of duty.

Activity 26 Gifts

Purpose

To show appreciation for the partners' contributions.

Approximate time

3–4 minutes per pair

Resources needed

Nil

Steps

Participants are asked to draw or describe in words the one gift that they would like to give their partner and the reason for that choice. The gifts can be abstract or concrete; for example, a job that uses your negotiation skills, time to go fishing, a bottle of fine wine.

Activity 27 Reviewing our relationship

Purpose

To stimulate reflective discussion on the relationship.

Approximate time

15 minutes

Resources needed

Reflective journal
Worksheet for each participant

Steps

Provide each participant with a worksheet for personal reflection. Use the reflective journal to record initial thoughts. Discuss these reflections with your partner.

Reviewing our relationship

In your role as a mentor or mentee identify any significant moment/s.

Describe what happened, why it was significant and what impact it had on you.

Where do you plan to go from here?

Activity 28 — Messages

Purpose

To personally and formally recognise the contribution of each participant.

Approximate time

Allow 5 minutes per pair plus 15 minutes

Resources needed

Nil

Steps

Pairs discuss with each other:
- What I really appreciated about my partner;
- Something I will do/am doing differently as a result of this partnership.

Each participant prepares a two-minute message to the whole group. This message can be anything related to the mentoring program. This could be a worthwhile moment that they would like to share, a particular insight, a word of warning or a funny incident.

Activity 29 — What role did you play?

Purpose

To stimulate a brief discussion around the key roles played by mentors at the different stages of the relationship.

Approximate time

15 minutes

Resources needed

Nil

Steps

Allow time for each pair to discuss the functions (to motivate, support, teach, counsel, promote, protect) that mentors perform, with examples from their own relationship.

Small groups then discuss: what was useful to the mentee; what prevented some functions from being performed; and what messages can be learned from this.

CHAPTER SIX

Additional Program Material

Checklists ● Sample Documents ● Proformas ● Other Tools

In this chapter I have provided a number of checklists, sample documents, proformas and other tools to assist program designers at each stage of the mentoring process. Assessing Organisational Readiness and Commitment, Program Design Checklists and Questions and Answers will be useful in the pre-program advertising and promotion stage. Background Information to This Project, Expressions of Interest and Application Forms will be used in the selection process. The Handbooks and Evaluations will be used during the program administration.

They should be used as a guide only. Your organisation will need to tailor its documentation to meet your specific needs and culture. It is much easier to modify the wheel than re-invent it.

Checklists

ASSESSING ORGANISATIONAL READINESS AND COMMITMENT

Use this pre-program checklist to clarify the purpose of your program, choose your target group, define outcomes and achievement measures. The questions can be used as a formal questionnaire, points to stimulate discussion during planning meetings or as an informal reflective tool for managers or team leaders contemplating introducing a mentoring program.

Needs assessment

Why do you want a mentoring program?
What specific needs will it address?
How were these needs determined?
What is currently happening to support these needs?
Will existing programs complement or compete with the mentoring program?
What major initiatives are occurring within the organisation now or planned for the near future?

Will these initiatives impact on the mentors or mentees?
Is this a pilot program?

Goals and outcomes

How are you defining mentoring?
Who will determine the program goals?
Are these short- or long-term goals?
What are the measurable outcomes for participants?
Who will determine when goals have been met?

Positioning the program

Who will act as sponsors, advocates or patrons of the program?
What unit is responsible for the program?
Who will be responsible for the program details?
What is their level of seniority?
What access do they have to influence and resources to support the program?
Is there an advisory committee?
What will be its role?
How will the program be advertised and promoted?

Resourcing

What resources are needed to accomplish the goals? Consider the following:
- Staff
- Time
- Administrative space
- Materials
- Venue

How will the resources be funded?
Who is responsible for obtaining the funds/resources?
Will the resources be part of a recurring budget?
Is the program dependent on a grant or submission?
Will participants be required to contribute to or pay the total cost of the program?
Is the program expected to be cost neutral?
Will an operating budget be designated for the program?
Who determines the amount of the budget and the allowable expenditure?
What staff will be needed?
Will the staff be acquired by contract, volunteer, loan, reallocation of duties?
How much and what kind of space is required for training and mentoring activities?
Does the training require participants or facilitators to travel long distances?

Co-ordination

How much planning time is required before the program begins?
At what time in the year will the formal program begin?
How much time has been allocated to orientation and training?
How long is the formal program expected to last?
What activities are considered part of the mentoring program?
How will the training activities be organised and scheduled?
How much flexibility is needed?
Who is responsible for co-ordinating the program?
What are their qualifications?
Does co-ordination of the mentoring program form part of their expected duties?
What access will the participants have to the program facilitator?

Participant selection and matching

Will participants be matched by the organisation or be identified as pairs?
How will mentees be identified—volunteer, nominated, membership of a defined group?
How will mentors be identified—volunteer, nominated?
Will the participants be screened?
How is the target group of mentees to be defined—new employees, aspiring leaders, managers in first twelve months of appointment?
Who will be responsible for screening pairs?
What criteria will be used to screen participants?
Who will match the pairs?
What criteria will be used to match pairs?
Will individuals have a choice in partner and/or the right to reject a match?
Will individuals have an option to change their partner if the match is not successful?

Setting expectations

What expectations have been set by the organisation? Consider the following.
- Time commitment
- Reports
- Tasks to be completed during the program
- Attendance at training

What training will be provided?
How will the mentors' contributions be recognised?
How will the mentors' mentoring skills be measured?
What expectations are set for mentees?
How will the program facilitator/designer communicate with pairs?
How will participants communicate with each other?
How will the formal mentoring be concluded?

Evaluation

What is the purpose of the evaluation?

Is the evaluation required for administration, to validate success, to obtain feedback from participants, for research?

Who will receive copies of the evaluation?

What will be evaluated—the mentor program design, training, orientation, role of facilitator, achievements of participants?

Has the organisation defined the expected outcomes from a successful program?

What evaluation instruments will be used—interview, survey, questionnaire, anecdotal data, reports?

Who will be included in the evaluation—mentors, mentees, program designer, facilitator, line managers?

When will the evaluations occur—following each phase, six/twelve months after the program conclusion?

Will the evaluations be used for program changes?

Who will analyse the evaluation data?

Who will have access to the assessment data on individual participants?

Who will receive copies of the evaluation reports?

PROGRAM DESIGN CHECKLIST

A useful checklist for program co-ordinators follows. It can be used as a guide or planning tool when organising and timetabling tasks to be completed and for checking that appropriate tasks have been completed by the due date.

PROGRAM DESIGN CHECKLIST

Promotion
Promotional literature includes the following.
- ❏ Sponsor's name and address
- ❏ Whether individual participants will need to contribute to the program costs
- ❏ Purpose of the program
- ❏ Benefits to participants
- ❏ Program format, content level and prerequisites
- ❏ Definition of the target group; for example, aspiring leaders, new leaders

Support materials
- ❏ Mentor handbook provided
- ❏ Mentee handbook provided
- ❏ Training workbook provided
- ❏ Relevant articles and professional reading available for participants

Policy
- ❏ Policy jointly determined by management and representatives of target group
- ❏ Policy guidelines outline specific goals, expected outcomes, content level, minimum time commitments
- ❏ Policy includes funding sources for co-ordinating personnel, facilitator/s, support materials, training venue and catering costs, print materials

Program personnel
- ❏ Program co-ordinator appointed
- ❏ Program facilitator and training presenter appointed
- ❏ Roles and responsibilities for program personnel documented

Participants
- ❏ Role and responsibilities for mentors clearly stated
- ❏ Role and responsibilities for mentees clearly stated
- ❏ Participants aware of the requirements of participating in the program

Selection
- ❏ Program given timely and appropriate promotion
- ❏ Promotional material includes characteristics of effective mentors and mentees
- ❏ Expression of interest sent to all in target group
- ❏ Voluntary participation encouraged
- ❏ Mentors and mentees encouraged to volunteer as pairs
- ❏ A range of mentor types is available

Matching

❑ Participants encouraged to nominate their own partner
❑ Individual mentees matched from a wide mentor pool
❑ Mentees and mentors given the right of refusal for proposed matchings

Orientation training

❑ Training program based on needs of participants
❑ Specific objectives and desired outcomes of each session clearly stated
❑ Variety of learning styles catered for
❑ Location and timing of training arranged to suit maximum number of participants
❑ Non-negotiable components of the program clearly stated and documented
❑ Relationship protocol agreement signed by all pairs
❑ Participants' preferred learning styles identified
❑ Individual learning plans developed for mentees
❑ Skills and experiences to be gained agreed

Relationship development

❑ Regular contact made by facilitator with each participant
❑ Facilitator available to support/counsel pairs
❑ Mid-cycle training session provides relevant skills training for pairs
❑ Pairs met at least the minimum number of times
❑ Meetings and specific activities evaluated and discussed by pairs
❑ No-fault divorce available
❑ Unsuccessful pairs receive counselling

Evaluation

Evaluation includes data on:

❑ Program promotion
❑ Selection
❑ Matching
❑ Orientation training
❑ Support material
❑ Role of facilitator
❑ Role of mentor
❑ Role of mentee
❑ Short-term goals
❑ Long-term goals
❑ Evaluation uses a variety of instruments; for example, questionnaire, interview, observation
❑ Data are sought from a variety of sources; for example, mentors, mentees, managers, facilitator
❑ Evaluation is conducted over a period of time
❑ Evaluation report is distributed to all participants, their managers, senior management
❑ Program outcomes are reported widely

Sample Documents

QUESTIONS AND ANSWERS

The following promotional material will be useful when advertising for prospective mentees, mentors, managers and sponsors. It could be used as the basis for an article on mentoring in your company journal, the framework for a talk on mentoring to a management group or a quick reference guide when answering commonly asked questions from interested mentors, mentees or their bosses.

What is mentoring?

Mentoring is a partnership between a more experienced person and someone new to a role or the organisation. This person is often called a mentee. The mentor teaches, counsels and provides psychological support and motivation for their mentee. They are usually outside the mentee's chain of command.

Many mentoring relationships are informal arrangements between two people with no support from or responsibility to anyone else. Structured or formal mentoring occurs when organisations initiate and support the mentoring processes.

The traditional mentoring model has been hierarchical and one-to-one, but new models are emerging such as peer mentoring and mentor hubs.

Is mentoring something new?

The concept of mentoring is timeless. The label 'mentor' came from The Odyssey, written by the Greek poet Homer. (Odysseus entrusted Mentor with the instruction and guidance of his son, Telemachus, while Odysseus was away during the Trojan War.) Mentoring is as relevant now as in Homer's time. As a personal and professional development strategy it is again being recognised.

What are the characteristics of effective mentees and mentors?

Effective mentors are those who are considered by the mentee to have specific job-related skills and expertise, highly developed interpersonal skills and a willingness to spend the time necessary to teach, counsel and provide support to someone else.

Effective mentees have a commitment to their own professional development. They will be prepared to take risks in their learning and try new approaches to solving problems.

What benefits can the mentee expect to receive from the program?

Mentees increase the likelihood of success and promotion within the organisation as a result of the targeted support that they receive in their developmental activities. They improve their skills and knowledge; increase their understanding of the organisation; develop a sense of perspective; and gain access to the mentor's professional network to some degree.

What benefits can the mentor expect to receive from the program?

Mentors experience an increase in job satisfaction and renewed motivation. They frequently develop a close relationship with their mentee who in some cases facilitates or even completes projects on their behalf. Mentors receive public recognition for their work, a sense of being needed and the opportunity to influence the career development of a talented young colleague.

What benefits can the organisation expect from sponsoring this program?

The organisation can expect increased productivity and enhanced performance of all participants in a mentoring program. Supported and planned induction programs and the renewed motivation of senior staff will ensure improved implementation of strategic and succession planning.

What am I committing to?

Insert here the commitments that each participant will be expected to make. These will include attendance at training programs, frequency and length of meetings with the mentor/mentee, products or projects completed as a result of participating.

What are some of the things mentors do?

Mentors perform a range of roles and take on many varied tasks. In the early stages of the relationship a mentor might motivate, teach and support their partner. As the relationship develops the mentor might also provide advice and counsel. Once confidence in the mentee's abilities has been gained, the mentor will also promote their mentee's skills and expertise in appropriate forums.

In order to do this mentors spend time with their partner. They might help the mentee in the development of their professional learning plans, conduct a performance appraisal, model specific leadership competencies, challenge and extend their mentee.

Where does the mentoring take place?

There is no fixed place for the mentoring function to occur. Each pair arranges a mutually convenient place to meet and plan. It is usual for both partners to spend some time visiting each other's workplaces. In shadowing programs the mentee would spend most of their time at their mentor's workplace.

What does the program facilitator do?

A facilitator is appointed to each program. Their role is to ensure that each person is gaining the most from their mentoring experiences. They will be in regular contact with each participant to hear how things are progressing. The facilitator might help pairs locate specific resources or contacts. The facilitator will ensure that each pair has established specific expectations and protocols.

What happens if problems arise with my partner?

Your program facilitator will be in regular contact with each pair. In the unlikely event of problems arising between you and your partner you can contact the facilitator and discuss these concerns confidentially. If the facilitator is unable to resolve your concerns your mentoring relationship with your partner will be discontinued. We call this a 'no fault divorce'. There will be no repercussions for either person involved.

Where can I obtain more information?

Insert appropriate details here.

BACKGROUND INFORMATION TO THIS PROJECT

Always provide promotional material specific to your program. The information here is a guide and needs to be adapted for each program that you organise.

Purpose of the program

Insert here the agreed purpose of your program, for example
To provide support for managers at the beginning of their first managerial appointment.

Program structure

Insert here a description of the program structure, for example
The program will be run in three phases:
1. Introductory phase, when the mentor matchings will be confirmed, individual guide lines established and skills in giving and receiving feedback will be developed.
2. Implementation phase, when the mentor–mentee pairs will work together on their agreed plan.
3. Review phase, involving a final training session and program evaluation.

Dates and times

Insert here a timeline for orientation and training, relationship development, and program conclusion.

Non-negotiables

Insert here the non-negotiable aspects of your program, such as attending all training programs, the minimum number of meetings between pairs, time commitments.

Venues

Insert here the location where all formal training will take place.

Costs

Include costs to participants. In some cases the organisation will be covering all costs; in other cases your organisation will pick up most costs and perhaps charge for catering; in some cases the sponsoring organisation is providing the infrastructure but the individuals will cover costs. It is rare to expect mentors to contribute financially.

Participants

Describe the target group and selection criteria.

Selection procedures

Describe your selection procedures: for example, all applicants will be accepted; applicants must nominate as pairs; mentees volunteer and will be matched to mentors by the organisation; or mentees choose from an attached list of approved mentors.

Completing your expression of interest

Include details for completion of the expression of interest such as closing date, return address, dates by which decisions will be made and the method of notifying successful and unsuccessful applicants. Contact telephone numbers should also be included for prospective applicants to seek further information prior to applying.

HANDBOOK FOR PARTICIPANTS

Once the participants have been selected, the fine tuning of the program can take place. Each participant will appreciate a program manual with information pertinent to them. The following provides a guide to the information to be included in a handbook for participants. A copy of the handbook should be made available to the mentor and mentee. It is the mentee's responsibility to complete appropriate documentation and maintain records.

Establishing expectations and guidelines for the partnership

We are voluntarily entering into a partnership. We expect that this relationship will have benefits for both of us. We want to maximise the time spent together. We have agreed on the following guiding principles for our interaction.

Confidentiality
Duration of the relationship
Meetings: frequency, location and duration
Responsibility for initiating contact
Where and when the partner can be contacted
Responsibility for setting agendas
Information required by the mentee
Information required by the mentor
Expectations of the mentee's boss
Expectations of the mentee of the mentor
Expectations of the mentor of the mentee
Main mentoring functions to be performed
Protocols for observing each other
Protocols for giving feedback

How to encourage risk taking in learning

Mentors can encourage risk taking in learning in the following ways.

- Exposing the mentee to as many experiences as possible
- Promoting question asking
- Listening willingly
- Being alert to the mentee's interests and needs
- Cutting red tape
- Sharing resources such as networks and experiences
- Introducing the mentee to contacts
- Establishing opportunities for team effort
- Providing constructive criticism from varied perspectives
- Finding appropriate audiences for the mentee's work
- Giving feedback
- Allowing for 'tag along' opportunities at conferences, meetings and other professional situations

- Creating opportunities for sharing feelings and reflections
- Acknowledging obstacles and facing them candidly
- Helping the mentee to recognise and accept the possibility of changes in plans or goals and thereby maintaining flexibility
- Maintaining a sense of humour during stressful times
- Keeping commitments
- Encouraging the mentee in new directions, once the established goals have been achieved

Role of the facilitator

A facilitator will be working with each pair. Previous participants have greatly appreciated the role that the facilitator played. Name has been chosen because of their depth and breadth of experience in leadership (insert appropriate terms here). The role of the facilitator is to support the interaction between the pair.

The facilitator could be asked to:
- provide personal support for either the mentor or the mentee;
- provide a link between the pair;
- ensure that appropriate goals are agreed prior to the mentoring;
- assist mentees to refine expectations so that realistic goals are achieved; and
- act as a mediator.

MEETING NOTES FOR MENTEES AND MENTORS

- Date
- Session number
- Time period of the session
- Main focus of the session
- Successes of the session
- Problems or difficulties encountered
- How did/could you resolve them?
- What do you need to do next?
- What specifically did you do to increase the success of this relationship?
- Time, date, location of next session
- Focus/expected outcome of next session

SAMPLE OUTLINE FOR RECORDING SHADOWING OBSERVATIONS

Date

Location where observations will occur

Context of observation
Background information that sets the scene for the observation

Focus of observation
The behaviours or skills specifically being targeted for observation

Observations
Record what occurred—do not make judgements

Positives
What you can gain

Points to raise as feedback
Observations that the mentor wishes to receive feedback on

Issues for discussion
Issues you want to pursue further

Proformas

EXPRESSION OF INTEREST—MENTEE

Many programs will call for expressions of interest. Your expression of interest form needs to take into account the final selection and matching processes that you will be using. The expression of interest form should be sent to all eligible applicants or widely advertised, asking eligible applicants to request an expression of interest form.

See page 116 for an example.

EXPRESSION OF INTEREST—MENTOR

The expression of interest form should be sent to all eligible applicants or widely advertised, asking eligible applicants to request an expression of interest form.

See page 117 for an example.

JOINT MENTEE/MENTOR APPLICATION

Some programs call for expressions of interest from self-nominated pairs from a target group. The expression of interest forms should be sent to all eligible applicants or widely advertised, asking eligible applicants to request expression of interest forms.

Use the individual mentee and mentor expression of interest forms, adding an extra page to each, with the following questions on it: What is your current relationship to your prospective mentoring partners? How did you identify your partner?

BOSS/SPONSOR NOMINATION FORM

Selection processes should include (but not exclusively) boss and sponsor nomination. Encourage managers to nominate members of their own team and potential mentees and mentors from other work units.

See page 118 for an example of a proforma for pairs or individuals to be nominated by the mentor's or mentee's boss or other sponsor.

PROGRAM EVALUATION

These proformas provide a framework to assist you to easily evaluate each stage of the program. Tailor them to your specific program.

See pages 119–121.

EXPRESSION OF INTEREST—MENTEE

Name
Work unit/location
Address
Telephone number
Email address
Length of time in the position
Qualifications
Manager
Telephone number
Email address
What do you consider to be your most significant achievements to date?

What do you hope to achieve by participating in the mentoring program?

What experiences would you like to have during the mentoring program?

What skills/knowledge/expertise can you offer your mentor?

Please indicate any of the following management competencies you would like to use as a focus for your own development.

❏ Clear thinking	❏ Power and influence	❏ Project management
❏ Personal organisation	❏ Conflict management	❏ Global perspective
❏ Stress tolerance	❏ Team building	❏ Environment and
❏ Communication	❏ Strategic planning	industry issues
❏ Personal awareness	❏ Corporate culture	❏ Leadership vision
❏ Supervision	❏ Resource management	❏ Public relations
❏ Developing others	❏ Program evaluation	

Do you have any particular constraints or requirements we need to consider when making a matching?

Please describe any previous involvement in formal or informal mentoring relationships.

EXPRESSION OF INTEREST—MENTOR

Name
Work unit/location
Address
Telephone number
E-mail address
Length of time in the position
Qualifications
Manager
Telephone number
E-mail address
What do you consider to be your most significant achievements to date?

What do you hope to achieve by participating in the mentoring program?

What skills/knowledge/expertise can you offer your mentee?

Please indicate any of the following management competencies which you see as strengths.

❏ Clear thinking	❏ Power and influence	❏ Project management
❏ Personal organisation	❏ Conflict management	❏ Global perspective
❏ Stress tolerance	❏ Team building	❏ Environment and
❏ Communication	❏ Strategic planning	industry issues
❏ Personal awareness	❏ Corporate culture	❏ Leadership vision
❏ Supervision	❏ Resource management	❏ Public relations
❏ Developing others	❏ Program evaluation	

Do you have any particular constraints or requirements we need to consider when making a matching?

Please describe any previous involvement in formal or informal mentoring relationships.

BOSS/SPONSOR NOMINATION FORM

Name
Work unit/location
Address
Telephone number
Email address
Name of nominated mentor and/or mentee
Work unit/location
Address
Telephone number
Email address
Describe your relationship with the mentor/mentee

Clearly explain your reasons for nominating this person/pair.

Have you discussed this nomination with the person/people involved?

PROGRAM EVALUATION—ORIENTATION

Initial advertising

Name

Date

How did you hear about this program?

Did the initial advertising and promotional material adequately and accurately describe the program?

Are you aware of people who would like to have been involved in this program but were unaware of its existence?

What further information could have been provided?

Selection procedures

Were the selection procedures clear and fair?

How can the selection process be improved?

How many people expressed interest and were not included in the final program?

How were the successful applicants chosen?

Were these processes known to all applicants?

How did unsuccessful applicants react?

What processes were put in place to support unsuccessful applicants?

Matching procedures

How many pairs self nominated?

How many pairs were matched by the organisation?

For pairs that were matched by the organisation, did the individuals have the opportunity to accept or reject their nominated partner?

Was there a pool of mentors for mentees to select from?

Did the mentees know all of the mentors in the pool?

If not, were mentees supplied with details of the mentors? If so, what information was included?

How was this pool nominated?

What criteria were used to match pairs?

Were any relationships terminated prior to the formal conclusion of the program? How were these pairs matched?

Orientation training program

Name

Date

Please rank the following on a scale of one to ten, with ten being the best possible score.

Trainer's knowledge of the subject
Trainer's presentation
Handouts/workbook
Learning activities
Pace
Venue
Please comment on any point that ranked one.
Which part of the program did you find most useful? Why?
Which part of the program did you find least useful? Why?
What are some of the new skills/knowledge that you have as a result of the session?
If you were designing this program how would you do it differently?
Do you have any other comments?

PROGRAM EVALUATION—MID-CYCLE

Mid-cycle training program

Use the same evaluation questions as for orientation training.

Support from program facilitator

How many times has the program facilitator contacted you?
What was discussed?
How many times have you contacted the program facilitator?
Why did you contact the program facilitator?
What benefit has the program facilitator role been to the mentoring program?
How could this role be improved?

Impact of the program

Name
Date
How many times have you met with your mentor/mentee since (insert date)?
Describe the main focus of these meetings.
Approximately how many telephone, facsimile or email contacts have you had with your mentor/mentee since (insert date)?
Describe the main focus of these contacts?
What do you value most about working with your mentor/mentee?
How could your relationship with your partner be improved?

PROGRAM EVALUATION—RELATIONSHIP CLOSURE

Relationship development

Name

Date

How many times have you met with your mentor/mentee since (insert date)?

Describe the main focus of these meetings?

Approximately how many telephone, facsimile or email contacts have you had with your mentor/mentee since (insert date)?

Describe the main focus of these contacts?

What did your mentor/mentee do to help establish an effective relationship?

Was the length of the formal program not long enough, just right, or too long? Please comment further.

What did you do to establish an effective relationship?

How did participating in this program assist in the development of your relationship with your mentor/mentee?

Did the program live up to your expectations?

What were some of the unexpected outcomes of the program (positive and otherwise)?

How can we improve this program?

PROGRAM EVALUATION—FOLLOW-UP

To be conducted twelve months after the conclusion of the program.

Name

Date

What contact have you had with your partner since the conclusion of the mentoring program?

Describe the focus of these contacts.

Describe the nature of your current relationship with your partner.

Describe how you see the relationship progressing/developing/changing over the next twelve months.

Other tools

APPRAISAL/COMPETENCY AUDIT

If you have not already conducted an appraisal or competency skills audit through your organisation there are a number of tools available from industry associations, training boards and commercial organisations. Associations and training boards provide industry-specific tools. There are generic competency profiles available that can be used to ascertain your skill level in management, leadership, service skills, team leadership and communication.

I have used the following two generic tools in a range of settings.

1. The MARC Management Competency Profile

The Management and Research Centre, MARC, is a division of the South Australian Training and Education Centre, based on the Salisbury campus of the University of South Australia. MARC has developed a Management Competency Profile which is easy to use, can be self administered or involve colleagues and managers in the process, giving a broader 360° view. The MARC Management Competency Profile has four layers. It is appropriate for use with base-level workers with leadership aspirations, introductory-level supervisors, middle-level managers and executives.

MARC also produces an Educational Leadership Profile suitable for use in schools and educational settings.

Both profiles are available from:
The Secretary
Management and Research Centre
PO Box 433
Salisbury 5108 Australia

2. Seven Dimensions Skills Indicators

Seven Dimensions produce a series of four skills indicators. These comprise Skills Indicators for Service, Team, Manager and Communication. Each indicator focuses on twenty specific skills. These indicators can also be used as self diagnostic tools or involve colleagues and managers to provide a 360° view. Each of the tools identifies strengths and areas that need to be developed.

Seven Dimensions Indicators are available from:
Seven Dimensions
8 Daly Street
South Yarra 3141 Australia

Both the MARC and Seven Dimensions tools are easy to administer, cost effective, and provide a rounded picture of skills and development needs.

PERSONAL LEARNING AND WORKING STYLES

There are a number of commercial instruments available that can be used to indicate personality and interpersonal styles and learning style preferences. Some indicators are self administering and available for purchase by any member of the public. The following two indicators have been widely used around the world but do require a qualified administrator.

FIRO B

The FIRO B is a leading indicator of interpersonal style. It measures how a person typically behaves towards others and how that person would like others to behave towards them.

It takes approximately 10 minutes to administer, either in a group or individually. It allows people to assess their own interpersonal style and the appropriateness of this style to the relationships they encounter. It is ideally suited to team building and development, individual development and counselling. It can be used by the pairs to help them to understand their own mentoring relationship better or in reflecting on other work relationships. This tool identifies some of the likely sources of compatibility or tension, improving communication, openness and trust and resolving conflicts. It is particularly effective at increasing self awareness and interpersonal effectiveness as part of the coaching process.

MBTI

The Myers-Briggs Type Indicator is commonly known as the MBTI. It is the most widely used personality instrument in the world. It is a forced choice self-report personality questionnaire, used to measure and describe people's preferences for how they like to get information, make decisions and orient their lives. The MBTI provides a simple way of seeing how people are alike and how they differ. I have used the MBTI in the orientation phase of a number of programs. The MBTI is a very effective tool to stimulate discussion around differences and similarities in personal styles—both working and relationships. I have found that the most successful mentor matchings are when there is some difference in type between the partners but some similarities as well.

NOTES